ULTIMATE GUIDE TO POKER TELLS

*Devastate Opponents by Reading Body Language,
Table Talk, Chip Moves, and Much More*

Randy Burgess

with Carl Baldassarre

TRIUMPH
BOOKS
CHICAGO

Library of Congress Cataloging-in-Publication Data

Burgess, Randy.
    Ultimate guide to poker tells : devastate opponents by reading body
    language, table talk, chip moves, and much more / Randy Burgess with
    Carl Baldassarre.
       p. cm.
    Includes bibliographical references and index.
    ISBN-13: 978-1-57243-807-1 (pbk.)
    ISBN-10: 1-57243-807-X (pbk.)
     1. Poker   I. Baldassarre, Carl. II. Title.

GV1251.B855 2006
795.412—dc22

2005031423

This book is available in quantity at special discounts for your group or organization. For further information, contact:

Triumph Books
542 South Dearborn Street
Suite 750
Chicago, Illinois 60605
(312) 939-3330
Fax (312) 663-3557

Printed in U.S.A.
ISBN-13: 978-1-57243-807-1
ISBN-10: 1-57243-807-X
Design by Patricia Frey
Cover photographs courtesy of AP/Wide World Photos

CONTENTS

ACKNOWLEDGMENTS

To the Boiceville school, for teaching me what poker is all about: Martha, Jimmy, Doug, Slide, Barry, Michael, and Robert. And to Carl, for his editing savvy and moral support.

—Randy Burgess

To Randy, who thinks he knows my tells. And to Marian, who does.

—Carl Baldassarre

The authors also would like to thank Adam Alster, Cary Cheung, Kenneth Cheung, Melissa Foerstman, Robert Goldman, Paul Kesselman, William Lui, Brian McNamee, Anthony J. Piantieri, and David Ryzhik for taking time away from playing to appear in the poker quiz photos. And special thanks to Brian for acting as our photographer.

INTRODUCTION

Do you need this book? See if you recognize yourself in one of the following descriptions.

♣ You're a casino regular, concentrating on playing tight but aggressively. You've read all the right books, you know how to calculate your odds and outs, but you're still barely staying ahead of the rake. A good player who's been fairly friendly has suggested you need to develop a better "feel." What the heck does *that* mean?

♣ You've been playing in a small no-limit cash game where some of the players take insane risks. These crazy players sometimes have big nights, but they often go broke. Sadly, you're not the one who gets their money. Instead, it usually goes to a small number of regulars who seem to have a sixth sense for when to call an all-in bet with no more than middle pair, or when to make a big laydown. How do they do that, you wonder, and how can you learn?

♣ You've always been an Internet player, but then last month a buddy got you into an underground club near your office. Now you've got serious information overload. All the loose chatter, facial tics, strange hand gestures, and attempts at gamesmanship that seem to verge on cheating—what should you pay attention to and what should you ignore?

♣ You're struggling to keep your head above water in a small-stakes home game, where the specialty of the house is various forms of high-low declare. The game's biggest winner is a disheveled former pilot with a bad rotator cuff, who seems to have mastered the art of declaring whichever way nobody else is going. He calls it "sliding," but can't explain how it's done. Can't—or won't.

In every one of these cases, learning how to recognize and interpret tells can help your game—sometimes a little, sometimes a lot. You'll benefit the most if you already play fundamentally sound poker, with at least some ability to read betting patterns. You'll benefit the least if you play like a train wreck, totally disregarding hand values and pot odds. If you're a novice, of course, you first need to learn proper strategy and gain experience at the tables—but even at this early stage, a knowledge of tells can be a valuable part of your basic training.

This book is perhaps the most complete resource available today for learning about tells. To make sure we didn't leave anything out, we not only worked from our own experience but ransacked poker literature for tips from such top players/authors as Bob Ciaffone, Doyle Brunson, Phil Hellmuth Jr., Dan Harrington, and T. J. Cloutier.

We've also included a special focus on today's most popular forms of poker: limit and no-limit hold'em. By contrast, the only other book devoted solely to tells, the otherwise classic *Book of Tells*, by poker legend Mike Caro, focuses mostly on draw poker—a game that's faded so thoroughly from the scene you'll probably never play it.[1] (If you're not a hold'em player, don't worry; we also cover other common games, including seven-card stud, Omaha Hi-Low, and more.)

This book makes clear what many books do not, but what every top player knows—that tells are valuable only in context, not in isolation. Reading a tell is like intercepting a coded message in wartime: even if you break the code, you still need to have a good idea of the enemy's strength, concerns, and plans in order for the message to make sense and affect what you do next.

With all of the books out there on poker psychology, there's been surprisingly little written on how people learn to interpret nonverbal signals—not just at the poker table, but in life in general. Among other things, we'll look at how certain highly trained police officers seem able to detect guilt or innocence in a flash, and, similarly, how some Buddhist monks can instantly detect concealed emotions such as fear or anger. Examples such as these lead us to methods for training your poker intuition that you might not have considered otherwise.

The plan of this book is simple. In the first couple of chapters, we'll lay a foundation by analyzing the nature of tells in general. Next, we'll go through a catalog of tells for specific games, since tells often vary from game to game. Finally, in the last few chapters, we'll discuss ways to improve your reading abilities, even as you strive to avoid giving off tells yourself. We'll also address an important related subject—how to protect yourself

---

[1] To be fair, Caro does include many classic hold'em and stud tells, such as the big stall with a big hand in no limit. (See chapter 5, "Tells in No-Limit Hold'em.")

against players who pretend to be broadcasting fake tells, but who are really crossing the line into angle-shooting and other unethical attempts at manipulation.

We also include a couple of appendices: a glossary to cover any poker terms you're not familiar with, plus a list of further resources for learning more about tells and about poker in general.

Tells may seem simple at first, but the more you learn about them, the more you realize how pervasive they are in any setting but online. The ability to gauge a player's nonverbal attitude and intentions is not a substitute for technical knowledge, but it *is* a helpful addition to your game—and it sure makes playing poker fun. And even for the pros, having fun is important. We hope you have fun reading this book, too.

CHAPTER 1

HOW IMPORTANT ARE TELLS IN POKER?

What's a tell? Following are a few short examples.

♣ In his prime, Doyle Brunson was perhaps the most feared no-limit hold'em player alive. But for a brief while he had a habit that would have made him easy prey for a keen-eyed opponent: when he was betting a real hand, he would count his chips before betting them; when he was bluffing, he would push his chips forward *without* counting them. Brunson's friend and fellow professional Amarillo Slim finally let him in on the secret.

♣ The most famous tell that never happened has to be Teddy KGB's cracking open of an Oreo cookie whenever he has a monster hand. Of course, you already know this—unless you're one of the 14 poker players on the planet who've never seen the movie *Rounders*, starring Matt Damon as the hero, Mike McDermott, and John Malkovich as the evil Teddy. In their climactic head-up hold'em duel, Mike finally catches on to the cookie tell and uses the knowledge to not only avoid losing his entire stack against Teddy's baby straight, but to put Teddy on tilt and turn the match around.

♣ Here's a tell of the sort I've witnessed time and time again, in one form or another. Again the game is hold'em, but instead of high-stakes drama, it's a $4/$8 limit game at a local club. Three average players are going through the motions: two early limpers versus a raiser on the button. The flop comes A♥T♦2♣; both limpers check, the button bets, and only the first limper calls. The turn brings a second Ten—and now the remaining limper flips up the corners of his hole cards to glance at them before again saying "check" in a voice that ever-so-slightly mixes boredom with disgust. The button bets and lo, the limper check-raises! The button is dismayed, but he shouldn't have been: there was no reason whatsoever for the limper to check his hole cards when the second Ten hit—unless he was doing a very bad acting job. If that weren't enough, the extra-bored voice should have been an additional tip-off.

This last example illustrates just why learning to interpret tells is so important, even if like most of us you're never going to star in a poker movie or play in the World Series of Poker. Becoming sensitive to the mélange of body language, acting, gestures, and facial expressions that make up tells can help any good player make fewer mistakes. You'll pay off less often when you're beat, fold less often when you're ahead, and in general develop a keen eye for opportunities either to make or save extra bets.

But it's not enough to grasp the general notion of tells and wing it from there. Poker is far more than just making or picking off bluffs based on your read of other players. You need to understand where tells fit in relation to other poker concepts: pot odds, implied odds, starting hand standards, game-specific strategy and tactics, and more.

The Truth about Tells

If you talk to professional poker players, many will say that movies like *Rounders* are bunk, and that tells really *aren't* that important when compared to other aspects of poker. But then, in discussing one hand or another, these same pros will casually mention that spotting a particular tell against a particular opponent helped them decide what to do—whether to bet, check, raise, or fold. So do we have a contradiction here, or not? The answer is, there's truth on both sides. Or to put it another way, tells are both vastly overrated and vastly underrated.

Tells Are Overrated

There are several reasons that tells aren't all they're cracked up to be in the popular imagination, whether that imagination has been fueled by movies such as *Rounders* or by televised tournaments such as the World Poker Tour or the World Series of Poker.

To start with, most casino poker is limit rather than no-limit, and tells are worth far less in a limit setting. To see why, imagine Mike McDermott and Teddy KGB playing $30/$60 limit hold'em rather than no-limit: Mike wouldn't have cared nearly as much how many Oreos Teddy fondled because his risk at any given point would be only another $60, not his entire stack. Teddy probably would have visited the dentist many times to have cavities filled before Mike caught on.

Another factor is that many of us play not just limit poker, but small-stakes limit poker to boot— games like $5/$10 hold'em or $10/$20 stud at the local club or casino. Such games tend to be loose and multiway, making the correct calculation of percentages more important than nearly any other factor. The prime requirement here isn't an exquisite ability to detect tells, but rather an aggressive odds-based strategy of the sort expounded upon in such newly minted classics as *Small Stakes Hold'em: Winning Big with Expert Play*, by Ed Miller (see appendix B, "Further Resources," for more information).

Even when it comes to reading opponents, it's more important to be good at reading betting patterns than it is to be good at reading tells. You can't have a poker hand without betting, whereas it's easy for a good player to suppress many, if not all, tells. As an exaggerated example, if you're playing seven-card stud and you know that Joe will always raise if he's got split Aces, but never raise if he has only an Ace-high three-flush, you've got a huge head start in knowing how to play him. I'd much rather have that information than a tell on him.

An additional caution is that if you spend most of your time watching for tells, you're liable to neglect other crucial aspects of your game. And that can make you play worse, not better.

Such considerations apply with equal force to no-limit and tournament poker. In nearly all cases, betting patterns give you the best handle on your opponents; and in nearly all cases, you've got to have a strong knowledge of the odds. For example, if you're short-stacked in a tournament and a big-stack player puts you all-in, you've got to know what hand values you should call with, based purely on the chips in play and the percentage chances of winning—tells have absolutely nothing to do with it.

As tournament pro Daniel Negreanu wrote in *Card Player Magazine*: "When you hear people talk about 'reading people,' what it really comes down to is reading into your opponent's mind what he is thinking at the moment, and trying to figure out how he would play various situations. . . . For the most part, a great player makes his read based on the actual betting that took place, not on facial tics."

Tells Are Underrated

And yet here's that same Daniel Negreanu, from that same *Card Player* article: "Having said all this [against tells], I should probably point out that what you say, or what you do with your eyes and hands, can be giveaways to the strength of your holding. Great players watch almost everything, and many do have an innate ability to read body language."

And here's Negreanu posting to his poker journal on his website, describing a tournament hand where his opponent, Kido Pham, might be holding a monster. Faced with a $50,000 river bet from Pham and holding only middle pair on a scary straight board, Negreanu tries to think through the action—in other words, he tries to read Pham's betting patterns. But that's no help, as the holding Pham is representing seems quite in character. Maybe it's time to fold.

But then Negreanu looks at Pham and notices something. "He looked stiff. Very stiff. He looked nervous and it didn't look staged." Negreanu calls the $50,000—and Pham promptly throws his hand in the muck instead of showing the bluff.

This isn't an aberration. Negreanu has numerous other posts in his journal where he makes one read or another to help him decide what to do. Other top players consistently describe the same scenario in their own accounts of big hands: although betting patterns and knowledge of the odds carry them most of the way, key decisions are often made based solely on the read of an opponent as strong or weak. Usually this read isn't made on the basis of a glaringly obvious tell, like twiddling a pinkie ring or eating a cookie, but as an overall impression of body language or facial expression.

Even in low-limit or small-stakes poker, tells can make a big difference if you weigh them appropriately. Why? Because they happen so often. As an analogy, imagine that you have an odd quirk—you always fold when you make four Aces. A horrible mistake, yet it wouldn't cost much in the long run since making four Aces is a rare event. Now imagine you have a different flaw in your game: you play too many hands. Each weak hand costs you only a fraction of a bet, but because you make this mistake so frequently, you're losing far more than you'll ever lose by folding quad Aces.

Each time you play a low-limit session at a club or a casino, you should be able to pick up reliable tells of one sort or another from as many as one-third of the players at the table within a half hour or so. Once you've acquired this information, it may or may not prove rewarding, depending on the players involved and the situations that arise. For example, if you have a tell on a loose-aggressive player who's in a lot of pots, it can be worth quite a bit if you catch some good hands against him. But if the players you've got tells on don't get into many pots, or if factors such as pot size consistently end up dictating your play, it won't make much difference.

Even so, you'll almost always run into situations during each sit where tells *do* matter. You'll be about to try a steal in hold'em, open-raising with KT in the cutoff, when a look to your left reveals that the button has a predatory gleam in his eye and a raise-sized stack of chips in his hand. Instead of stealing, you quietly muck. Or you'll be pondering whether to fold to an unexpected turn bet when you notice your opponent is nervously jiggling her leg under the table—a tell you spotted earlier and correlated with a bluff. Instead of folding, you now raise.

If you don't want to take my word for it, how about the word of Roy Cooke? If you don't yet know of Cooke, you should; he's a regular columnist for *Card Player*, and his descriptions of the thought process of a top pro flow-charting his way through hands should be an essential part of anyone's poker education. According to Cooke, reading Mike Caro's *Book of Tells* early on sensitized him to the idea of tells. As a result, Cooke often picks up on giveaway mannerisms or behaviors to which other players remain oblivious. "I have made a lot of profit from tells in my years at the table," he concludes.

Context Is Everything

You're in the middle of a hand, when suddenly you notice something different about your opponent's behavior or demeanor—in other words, you pick up a tell. What do you need to be thinking about to make use of this tantalizing yet potentially misleading scrap of information? For a start, I'd suggest the following.

♣ Your opponent's level of poker knowledge. For example, a naïve beginner who can't properly judge the value of her own hand may give you a tell that she's stronger than she really is because she overrates her hand. The same tell coming from a more experienced player would be much more useful.

♣ The relative narrowness or width of your opponent's hand selection—not just his starting hands, but what hands he'll continue with under pressure. Loose opponents play more hands, so they're harder to read than tight opponents. Loose-aggressive opponents are the hardest to read of all from the point of view of hand-reading, but tells pick up value against them since they get involved in so many pots and are more likely than the average player to be bluffing.

♣ Overall betting patterns based on all of the above factors. For example, in stud, how often will he value-bet the river with two small pair or an unimproved big pair when head-up? In hold'em, does he tend to slow-play or fastplay hands like sets and two pair? Which conditions influence his decision?

♣ Whether he's an actor or not. More on this in the next chapter, when we begin to separate tells into categories.

♣ How other aspects of the hand align. For example, if the pot is huge compared to the size of the bet, you have to be super-sure of a tell that says you're beaten before you can justify a fold. You'll hardly ever be that certain, so usually you'll call. Another thing to be wary of is locking in too much on a single player in a multi-way pot, to the extent you forget that there are other players in the hand.

Say you take all of this into account, and after some quick thinking you're convinced the tell is valid: your opponent has a hand other than the one he's representing or that hand-reading logic would suggest he holds. Even now, the tell is only useful if it gives you information that *changes* your decision. If you were going to fold anyway, a tell that your opponent is strong does you little good. But if you were intending to call, then the tell helps you a lot. Or it can be the reverse, as in Negreanu's case—he was intending to fold, but the tell helped him to make a great call.

Tells According to Game Type

Interestingly, the manner and number of tells depend on the type of game involved, not just the players or the betting structure.

♣ For whatever reason, subconscious chip-grabbing with good starting cards is much more common on Third Street in seven-card stud than before the flop in hold'em. Another tell that occurs more often in stud than in hold'em is shuffling down cards when on a draw. Card-shuffling does occur in hold'em, but it's more of an individual tic and thus harder to interpret.

11

♣ Some games just generate more tells, period. The best example is Mike Caro's favorite game, draw poker. Tells infested draw to a degree never seen before or since. With only two rounds of betting, players developed all sorts of shticks to try to convince other players they were weak before the draw when they were actually strong, so as to lure them in; likewise, when they were weak, they would act strong so as to forestall raises and get better odds for drawing. Mason Malmuth, a well-known poker writer, has written that tells were such a big part of draw that when he switched from that game to hold'em, "it seemed like someone had suddenly 'turned the sound off.'"

Summing up, I think it's obvious that tells *do* have enormous value in poker—but only when used wisely. In the next chapter, we'll lay another brick in the foundation when we examine the physical stuff tells are made of.

CHAPTER 2

THE ANATOMY OF TELLS

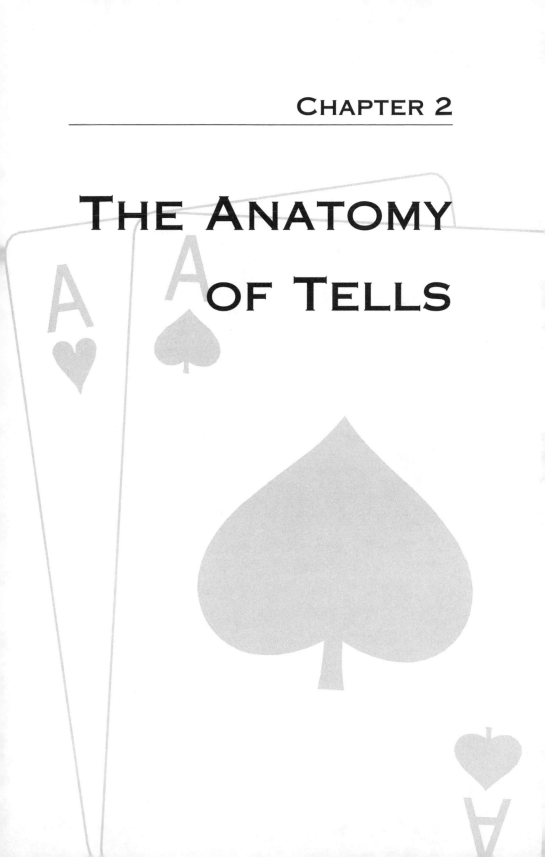

You already know that tells consist of things like body language, facial expressions, gestures, and so on. But as it happens, we can be quite a bit more specific about the nature and origins of these various signals. There are several good reasons to do so.

First, many tells are based on physiological reactions that lie either partly or wholly outside our control. Such involuntary tells apply to all types of poker; an example would be uncontrollably trembling hands when you bet a monster such as a straight flush in a huge pot. We'll discuss this category of tells in detail in this chapter.

Second, for tells that potentially *are* under our voluntary control, we need to distinguish players who are genuinely displaying these signals from those who are feigning them. Like involuntary tells, acting jobs are common to all poker games; by introducing the concept here, we'll be able to refer back to it later on. An example of an acting tell is when a player slams down his chips to appear strong when betting with a weak hand.

Third, this chapter will introduce an obvious but important concept: the difference between *generic* tells and *individual* tells. Generic tells are what we'll discuss in the next few chapters. They're the type of tell that occurs so often you can recognize it in somebody you're playing against for the first time. Once again, an easy example is chip-grabbing with a good starting hand in seven-card stud.

The idea behind an individual tell, on the other hand, is self-explanatory: it's a tell peculiar to an individual player, rather than to many players. We've all got our individual tells. It can be something as commonplace as a quickly concealed smile when you hit a good card, or as strange and unique as a particular way you have of nervously flipping your fingers against your cards when you're holding a monster. The point is, individual tells aren't as instantly recognizable for what they are as generic tells, so they have to be hunted out. In this chapter I'm going to tell you what to focus on to make the hunt easier.

An example of a good place to look for individual tells is chip-handling: many of us subconsciously handle our chips one way when we're betting a strong hand and a completely different way when we're betting or calling with a weak hand. And we're not even vaguely aware of it. I've displayed a chip-handling tell myself on occasion; I never noticed until an attentive buddy pointed it out to me.

Involuntary Tells

Our involuntary reactions tend to be the result of stress and strong emotion—our heritage as stick-bearing primates in an eat-or-be-eaten world. We betray our fear of holding a losing hand the same way we once betrayed our fear a lion might snap us up on the savanna: our heart rate speeds up to prepare us to run away or to attack, and blood flow increases to our legs for the same reason. There's nothing we can do about it because these reactions are wired into our autonomic nervous system. And while no one can see the blood rush to our legs at the poker table, it *is* possible for an opponent to study the pulse at our neck to see if it speeds up. I've never made use of this particular tell, but Doyle Brunson mentions it in his classic book *Super/System* as one of the key things he looks for to see if a player might be bluffing. I've even heard of a player going so far as to reach across the table to feel the pulse in an opponent's neck while considering whether or not to call an all-in wager. If someone tried this on me, I'd probably put them in a wristlock and call the floor.

Another characteristic sign of tension occurs when our voice tightens up, getting slightly higher in pitch, or even cracking if we're really nervous. This is one of the reasons (there are others, as we'll see) that no-limit players often pester their opponents with questions if they suspect they're bluffing.

Although these tells are highly reliable when they occur, their absence isn't necessarily significant. In other words, just because someone doesn't seem tense, you can't necessarily conclude that they've got the goods. Among other things, the more poker you play, the more jaded you get, and thus the higher the stakes have to be before you actually tense up in a tight situation. In addition, there are some players (especially in no-limit) who find bluffing enjoyable, even exhilarating. They don't tense up when bluffing the way most people would, and that can make them very dangerous.

The opposite of feeling jeopardized, of course, is feeling utterly confident of victory. In such cases, we tend to relax, and our voices and bodies will reliably signal this. Typical signs of confidence at the poker table include a deeper voice than usual, an erect but relaxed posture, and precise but assured movements.

I often notice such signals of utter relaxation in home games, where various forms of high-low poker make lock hands a routine occurrence. A player with a mortal lock often becomes visibly bored with the proceedings, tossing his chips into the pot like a robot as he raises. With the outcome no longer in doubt, the hand has become anticlimactic to him, and he can't be bothered to conceal it. This is especially true of action-seeking players, who seem to enjoy chasing long shots more than they do actually winning.

Other involuntary tells occur with facial expressions, gestures, and postures. But because these can sometimes be faked, albeit dubiously, we need to learn first about acting.

Poker Psychology and the Evolution of Actors

When it comes to poker, we can choose just to play our cards, or we can liven things up with a little show, hoping to con our opponents out of more money. But not everyone chooses to act, and not everyone even knows that acting is a choice. The factors at work include how long we've played, our personality, how skilled a player we've become, and whether we believe acting is worth all that effort.

Another way to structure this is to consider that we all follow the same path up the mountain in learning how to use deception in poker—it's just that most of us never make it to the summit, from lack of either skill or will.

Stage 1: When we're just starting out, we usually don't bother to conceal our delight in a strong hand or our disappointment in a weak one. Hey, it's a triumph even to be able to tell the difference!

Stage 2: Soon enough we learn to keep quiet about our monster hands so as not to scare off customers—the beginning of a poker face. We're still usually pretty transparent about our weak hands, though—we don't yet realize that even a weak hand is sometimes the best hand.

Stage 3: In the next stage, we become actors. We'll start complaining out loud about how crappy our hand is when really we hold a straight flush, or we'll throw our chips hard into the pot to give the impression our four-flush is really a made flush, in hopes everyone will fold. Most low-limit recreational players stay stuck at a mix of Stages 2 and 3, by the way.

Stage 4: Smart players who continue to study the game soon realize that acting is hard work. Opting for a simpler approach, they try to minimize tells by always behaving the same way—Vulcan poker. Interestingly, these smart players often neglect to do any tell-reading of their own, beyond certain minimal basics. They prefer instead to concentrate on reading hands by reading betting patterns. It's a smart strategy, but as we discussed in chapter 1, an incomplete one.

Stage 5: Elite players who move up to big-stakes and no-limit games still rely on the skills they learned in Stage 4—but in addition, the reading of tells through body language, voice, and other cues becomes important. Such players learn to literally think like their opponent, even as they learn to manipulate opponents by broadcasting reverse tells, fake signals designed to get opponents to bite on a read that's pure baloney. This is where strong no-limit players and tournament superstars like Gus Hansen and Annie Duke hang out. It's all bluff, all the time—until you finally decide to start calling those bluffs, at which point they show you the nuts.

Caro's Law of Tells

One of the first experts to describe Stage 3—poker players as actors—was Mike Caro, a specialist in draw poker as played in the cardhouses of Gardena, California. As I mentioned in the introduction, Caro became fascinated enough with tells to write the first book to treat the subject at length, originally published in 1984 as *The Book of Tells* and since reprinted under a variety of titles.

The book is mostly photos of tells from draw poker, but in his introduction, Caro elucidates what he calls his Great Law of Tells: "Players are either acting or they aren't. If they are acting, then decide what they want you to do and disappoint them."

Even more important is Caro's observation that when players are acting, they tend to follow a simple rule: if they're strong, they try to appear weak; if they're weak, they try to appear strong.

Knowing this rule alone will give you a tremendous advantage at the poker table, given the number of recreational players who like to ham it up, but do so with a total lack of imagination. As Caro suggests, you'll often want to do the opposite of what the actor wants you to do. If he wants you to fold, consider calling or raising; if he wants you to call, lean toward folding unless your hand has concealed strength. But keep in mind what I said in the previous chapter about context: you really need to access all the information available to you before you can properly interpret any tell.

The other interesting thing about Caro was that although his persona as a poker author was coolly rational, his nickname as a player was "Crazy Mike." At times he pretended to be a lunatic at the poker table, with such tricks as raising on a garbage hand, then showing it down for all to see, laughing wildly. Such shenanigans made it hard for opponents to put him on a hand, a strategy we'll talk about more in chapter 8, "Avoiding Tells Yourself."

Involuntary Tells That Can Be Acted— Sometimes

We've made a neat distinction between involuntary tells on the one hand and acting jobs on the other. However, there's a wide and foggy no-man's land stretching in between these two extremes. Here we find two very common categories of tells: facial expressions and body language. You can fake a facial expression, all right, but with a few exceptions, a sufficiently skilled interpreter can usually see through to the real emotion underneath. You can fake your body language, too, though this is a little less common.

Facial Expressions and Micro Expressions

Stage 3 players, those who've gotten to the point where they spend a lot of time acting, generally aren't very good at producing misleading expressions. What they mostly manage to produce are exaggerated emotional displays—for example, a cartoon of disgust as they look at their secretly terrific river card. Even the average opponent can see through such displays. But since the average opponent typically also plays bad poker, it often doesn't make much difference: the supposedly disgusted player bets or raises and still gets the callers he wants. This theater of the absurd is played out hand after hand at low-limit tables in casinos across the country.

Someone who's actually paying attention, however, can begin dissecting these big facial expressions according to Caro's Great Law of Tells. The vulnerability of the bad actor is one reason why Stage 4 players no longer bother to act themselves: they figure it's just not worth the effort, especially as they move up in stakes and find that most of their new opponents have seen it all before.

Just why *are* facial expressions so hard to fake? For one thing, a lot of very complex musculature is involved for purposes most of us can't begin to keep track of. There are literally thousands of distinguishable facial expressions, many of which have nothing to do with emotion, but instead serve as a means to emphasize speech, or else to convey speech-like responses. Our faces can do amazing things, but most of us aren't trained actors, so we can only do these amazing things when it's natural to do so—not on command.

It was also important during human evolution that we be able to communicate dense amounts of information quickly and reliably, and the face helps us do that. If we'd been able to easily conceal emotions whenever we wanted to, we'd have been unable to form the bonds of trust that led to hunter-gatherer bands and eventually to tribes.

Finally, few of us get much practice at complex facial deception in real life; the poker table, with its brief moments of high drama, is the exception, not the rule. Regardless of how bad a real-life conflict gets, we generally allow our faces to convey at least some of what we're feeling.

All of this leads us to an extremely tantalizing fact: because of all this hardwiring, even the straightest of poker faces is still prone to leaking fractions of emotions. These leakages are called *micro expressions*. They typically occur when a surprising event catches us momentarily unprepared, as when a miracle card makes us a huge hand or an opponent raises when we thought he'd just call. Few of us are skilled at reading micro expressions, for the same reasons we're not skilled at concealing them, but it's an ability that *can* be developed. It's my guess that a player like Phil Hellmuth Jr., known for his uncanny ability to make accurate reads of strength or weakness, is most likely making use of micro expressions, even if not by that name.[1] We'll explore this topic more in chapter 7, "Becoming a Poker Psychic."

Posture and Gestures

Reading posture as a tell is for the most part reading obvious body language: for example, a player who slumps

---

[1] In fact, not by any name. Hellmuth is famous for not being able to explain his great reads; all he can say is that he "just knew."

in dejection may not like his hand. But you've got to know him well enough to know if he's acting. A big slump is more likely to be an act, a barely visible slump is more likely to be truthful.

Here, too, we leak information we're not aware of. Studies have found that outside of poker, our posture or even our gestures may reflect emotions we know we're feeling but would rather not display. For example, if our boss is belittling us during a confrontation in the privacy of his office, we may subconsciously give him the finger the entire time. (Filmed experiments have caught exactly this sort of behavior from perfectly respectable people.) Very likely, our boss will be as unaware of this hostile gesture as we are. Or we may make a half-shrug when asked a question we'd prefer not to answer; because it's such a subtle movement—perhaps using only one shoulder, and with a minimal degree of movement—it's much harder to catch. And very likely we'll make this movement while averting our body, rather than presenting ourselves frontally as we normally do when we want to encourage clear communication.

At the poker table, encounters are usually over with more quickly than in a real-life argument, so there's less time for half-concealed postures and gestures to develop. But a trained observer can still catch leakages of this sort, especially in no-limit, where players are allowed to take as long as several minutes to make a big decision. A fascinating example of this comes from the second season of the World Poker Tour, in a no-limit hand at the Bay 101 Shooting Stars final table between Scott Wilson and Phil

Gordon: Wilson raises preflop with AK but misses the flop, and Gordon starts playing back at him. As Wilson ponders whether to call Gordon's turn bet, both his posture and his facial expression start to disintegrate. He twists his body away from Gordon in discomfort, drops his chin onto his hands as his neck muscles slacken, and smiles in painful embarrassment. He can't help any of this behavior.

The desire to keep such postural tells to a bare minimum is one reason why many no-limit tournament players train themselves to freeze into immobility during big hands. Chris "Jesus" Ferguson is one of these: at times he seems little more than a stick figure made up of a cowboy hat, shades, and steepled forearms. A fair number of recreational no-limit players like to use this trick, too, but unless a lot of money is involved, it tends to look sillier than on TV. And it's not strictly necessary—watch a fidgety player like Gus Hansen and try to tell when he's bluffing or not based on his body language!

Hunting for Individual Tells

To remind you, some tells are common to many players; these we call generic tells. Others are unique to a given individual, so we call them individual tells. An example of the former would be shuffling your down cards when you're on a draw in seven-card stud; an example of the latter might be a player who twists his mouth sideways and looks you in the eye whenever he's caught a big hand. (Ivan, if you're reading this, that's your tell.)

Both types of tells are valuable, but in slightly different ways. Generic tells are useful because they're so common and easy to recognize; individual tells are often harder to spot, but are highly reliable when you find them. When Stage 3 actors try to fake tells, they're generally attempting to replicate generic tells. Great no-limit players, on the other hand, are more likely to try to fake individual tells, knowing that opponents at that level are more likely to watch for these and be convinced by them.

An example of a fake individual tell comes from *Super/System*: Brunson writes that on occasion, he'd repeat a phrase like "Gee whiz" every time he bluffed. When he was finally caught at one of these bluffs, he'd wait until he had the nuts—then he'd once again say "Gee whiz," hoping to trap some proud observer into donating all his chips. Of course, Brunson was probably saying something considerably more pungent than "Gee whiz."

Individual tells tend to be organized around a few key areas of behavior, so you want to look in those areas regularly as part of your tell-hunting routine. Following are the top candidates.

Chip-Handling

This category of individual tell is a favorite of many pros', including Bob Ciaffone and Dan Harrington. As Ciaffone notes, it's easy to keep a poker face, but very few people are smart enough to keep "poker hands." That makes this tell highly reliable when it occurs.

As I've already mentioned, many of us handle our chips one way when we've got an ordinary hand, and another way entirely when we've got a big hand. And we may handle our chips yet another way when we're bluffing.

Therefore, it pays to spend as much or more time watching your opponents' hands as their faces.

Here's a quick example of a chip tell I recently witnessed during a baby no-limit game at a private club. A very conservative player had gotten involved in a head-up hand in an unraised pot. He was in early position, out of the big blind, and on the flop he just checked and called the button's pot-sized bet. The turn card arrived, a baby that paired the board, and again Mr. Conservative checked. The button bet about double the pot, so things were starting to build.

And now our hero did a strange thing: calling this bet, he didn't place his chips in neat stacks, as he usually did; instead, he flipped them off his cupped fingertips, a little like a grandfather chucking a baby's chin. To me, watching, it was like someone had pulled the fire alarm, even though no one else seemed to hear it. The flurry of action on the river saw the button go all-in, to his grave disadvantage: the turn card had given Mr. Conservative four-of-a-kind, crushing the button's full house. The odd chip motion might well have suggested trouble to a top player, but went unnoticed by his opponent.

Eyes

The eyes are so important to our intentions that players at all levels often try to conceal them, wearing sunglasses or a hat with a brim (or both, à la Chris Ferguson). This may appeal to you as well; we'll cover the subject more fully in chapter 8.

Of special importance is where a player is looking during a hand. In a high-low game, for example, he may study an opposing low hand if he's thinking of going low—but only if he's naïve enough to let his eye movements be captured. Many high-low players develop at least some notion of eye fakes to avoid this. A more reliable indicator is when a player stares at the pot for a long while as he counts it; additional clues are if his head bobs or his lips move. Most likely he's on a draw and is seeking to calculate his pot odds.

Verbal Tells

An opponent who's excited about his hand may become suddenly talkative and start chattering away about anything and everything under the sun. On the flip side, some players will start yapping at you when they have a weak hand and don't want you to bet. By making insinuations or talking tough, they hope to bamboozle you into giving them a free card.

An interesting variant is when a player who's usually fairly quiet starts urging other players to hurry up or impatiently asks who the action's on. He's got a good hand—maybe a very good hand. This tell applies more to weak players than strong players; strong players feel that same urge to hurry things along so they can make whatever move it is they're planning, but they're better at keeping their mouths shut.

Lastly, you'll occasionally encounter a very talkative player who loves to dominate the conversation at the table—until he catches a good hand, at which point he clams up and concentrates on playing. This is a highly reliable indicator when it occurs.

Betting Patterns

This last tell might not seem like a tell; after all, didn't I say in chapter 1 that betting patterns are distinct from tells?

Well, yes and no. It's true that observing an opponent's starting cards and how he prefers to play certain types of hands is a separate subject from tells in general; but it's also true that some bets cry out so clearly that it's as if your opponent had turned his cards face up right there and then.

A good illustration of this comes from seven-card stud. Certain betting structures allow the bet size to double on Fourth Street once anyone's doorcard is paired. It happens that there are some players who will always make this double bet when they pair up but *haven't* actually made trips—they're hoping to scare people out when actually they hold a weak hand. These same players often will bet the small bet when they do trip up, hoping to suck opponents in. It's part of a pattern of trickiness on their part. Once you know this about them, it's as good as a tell. And it feels like a tell, too, because of the way it jumps out at you. Unlike most instances of hand-reading, no painful thought is required.

CHAPTER 3

FIRST IMPRESSIONS

Like most of us, I tend to assume I'm pretty good at capturing the essence of someone when I meet them for the first time; how else could we get by in life if we didn't have this ability to take a quick mental snapshot? Too often, though, these snapshots are really a reflection of ourselves and our assumptions, not what's actually in front of us. This goes double for poker.

One particular first encounter is seared into my mind. It occurred early in my card-playing career, when I was just starting to get cocky about all the studying I'd done and my newfound ability to beat the game. At the time, I was playing $1–$3 spread-limit stud with no ante—the first casino poker I ever experimented with. Today it seems ludicrous, but back then I thought it was the real deal, compared to the nickel-dime-quarter home games I'd played in for so long.

So here I am sitting in a stud game at Foxwoods Casino in eastern Connecticut, playing in my best Roy West style—much tighter than anyone else at the table, but aggressive when I do come into a pot. (If you've never read Roy West, he's the author of the best low-limit stud book available.) Now this Asian guy joins the table.

Right away I'm on my guard. First, he's young and huskily built, two things that suggest he might be more aggressive than the usual assortment of retirees who make up most of the table. Second, he *is* Asian—and I've just read in Mike Caro's *Book of Tells* that Asians at the poker table are either "very skillful" or "very luck-oriented." Either way, I have to be wary of him, right?

On his very first hand, he raises my split Aces on Third Street with just a Seven showing. Based on nothing more than my impression of his heavy build and his youth and Caro's advice about Asians, I immediately decide he's trying to run over the table. I play back with a full $3 reraise to show him I can't be bullied. Fourth Street goes the same way. On Fifth Street I make Aces up and have full confidence I'm winning. I even feel sorry for him, especially on the river when he just calls instead of raises. Then he shows me the trip Sevens he started with and sweeps in the pot.

"Dealt that way—rolled up," he says happily. For the rest of his sit he proceeds to play a passive, nondescript game, never jamming the way he did against me with his trips.

Oops.

Obviously, I'm telling you this story for a reason. This chapter is about sizing up new opponents as quickly as you can, so as to give yourself a head start in taking their chips. But that sizing up shouldn't consist of indiscriminate stereotypes and muddled thinking. The fact is, stereotypes of the sort suggested by Caro are even less true today than they were then. There are different attitudes toward gambling based on culture, gender, age, and so on, as we'll see; but you need to observe someone quite carefully before you decide whether they fit a particular norm. Even then, other kinds of evidence can be far more useful and far less prone to error.

Why Do First Impressions Matter at All?

During a four-hour sit in a public cardroom, it's not uncommon for the entire table aside from yourself to turn over two or three times. Just as you get to know a player fairly well, he's gone and you've got to start over with his replacement. That puts a premium on the ability to make reasonable guesses at playing style based on circumstantial evidence.

Naturally you'll adjust these guesses as you begin to observe more concrete details such as the number of hands he plays, what hands he actually shows down, and so on. The point is to start forming your evaluation the moment he joins the table, rather than wait. It's seat-of-the-pants poker, but what poker isn't?

Race, Gender, Age, and Other Non-Poker Cues

Let's tackle stereotypes first. Some are truer than others.

Asian players. Mike Caro isn't the only poker writer to assert that Asians of both sexes are often loose-aggressive gamblers, betting and raising with abandon and happily chasing draws despite terrible odds. But in the New York City area, where I play a lot, most of the Asian American players I meet don't fit this stereotype. They're usually very Americanized, and their play reflects the variety you'd expect. On the other hand, many Asians with heavy accents do seem unusually luck-oriented. And there are plentiful accounts of heavy gambling being taken for granted in countries including China, Taiwan, Vietnam, and Hong Kong. Just be sure to consider the individual as well as the cliché.

Women. The standard line from poker writers is that women play less aggressively than men: they bluff less, they raise less, and so on down the line. If you fancy yourself a sociologist, you might speculate that women play this way because they want to be liked more than they want to win. While all of this may be true, I've never found it very helpful. Women make up such a small percentage of poker players that I find it better to deal with them on a case-by-case basis rather than generalize. That way I won't be ambushed when the gal on my right turns out to be a better player than I am. I will say that I've never once encountered a loose-aggressive female player—but I'm sure they exist.

Players with jewelry or tattoos. Another standard line: players who flaunt such decorations tend to be superstitious, and thus prone to gambling it up. In this case I thoroughly agree. Said player may be a loose-aggressive steamer, a loose-passive calling station, a confirmed bluffer, or what have you, but he's almost always determined to get his money in the middle of the table as fast as he can. I think the reason this indicator is so reliable is that it depends on personality more than culture. However, even here you should be cautious: both body piercing and tattooing are on the rise, so a young man with a nose ring, for example, could just as easily be a rock as a maniac.

Senior citizens. As we age we tend to play more conservatively. So says poker writer Bob Ciaffone, who ought to know, being in his midsixties himself. However, I regularly encounter some very pugnacious, loose-aggressive senior players on the New York City club scene. Remember, too, that the definition of elderly has been pushed back as baby boomers have aged and the state of medicine has improved. Better to use your prejudices about aging as a goad to get yourself to see an older opponent more clearly as an individual. You'll play better against him and you'll enjoy yourself more, too.

Successful businessmen. You've probably heard that millionaire businessmen like to splash around at the high-stakes tables. Well, at the slightly lower limits where most of us play, it's a bit different. It's true that prosperous businessmen (the owner of a chain of candy stores, a wine merchant, an Internet entrepreneur, etc.) often prefer to buy in for the maximum in middle-sized games. And because they've been successful in life, they generally exude self-confidence, a quality that at first blush might make you think they're going to be a force at the table.

But don't let their supposed mojo throw you. Usually they haven't put in the time to learn to play poker well, and it quickly shows. They tend to not be very aggressive, despite all those chips in front of them. When they *are* aggressive, it's often confined to starting-card play—for example, putting in an extra raise before the flop in hold'em. That's easy to do. But once the flop hits and they actually have to play poker, they tend to revert to more passive ways unless they catch a monster.

Initial Clues to Inexperience
or Lack of Skill

Small buy-ins. Someone who buys in for fewer than 25 or 30 big bets in a limit game hasn't given themselves enough chips to play well given the inevitable ups and downs. It's a sign they don't understand the concept of variance, and are either inexperienced, unskillful, or both.

Players may also buy in for a short stack because that's all they can manage at the moment. If so, they're probably a losing player, addicted to poker but unable to build a bankroll.

You might expect a small stack to play tightly, especially if the player is nervous, inexperienced, or can't afford a rebuy. But when it comes to starting hand selection, often this isn't the case: if the player doesn't understand something as fundamental to poker as variance, he also likely doesn't understand much about starting hand values and will end up playing too many hands.

Where a short stack is more likely to play tight is on later streets. If you pick your spots, you can probably bluff him off hands he'd think about calling with if he had more chips. The exception is in no-limit, where a short-stacked player inevitably reaches the point that he's got so few chips he stops caring. At that point he's unbluffable because he figures he's ready to go home anyway.

A small-stack player who's a consistent loser in no-limit will occasionally prove to be a wild, reckless gambler. That's why he's got the small stack in the first place: he's the sort of player who will occasionally have a huge night, but the next night go home broke. His only hope of playing with a full buy-in on a regular basis is to get a high-paying day job.

Finally, you may very occasionally run into a short-stack player who knows what he's doing. This applies only to no-limit cash games, where being short-stacked can actually be an advantage against loose, weak opponents. Such a player will be supertight preflop, playing only very good hands and always raising with them. He'll tend to get the rest of his tiny stack in on the flop or turn, minimizing his opponents' implied odds and bluffing chances. He's a totally different animal than the other short-stack players we've been talking about—but other cues about him will probably have alerted you to this already.

Chip-stacking. At least one poker authority has written that players who stack their chips neatly are more likely to be conservative, and can therefore be bluffed more easily. This is pure baloney; maybe it was true 20 years ago when poker was less popular, but it's certainly not true today. Careful chip-stacking doesn't necessarily correlate to much more than a desire to keep count. In limit, few players good or bad strew their chips about carelessly. In no-limit, virtually all experienced players keep their chips neatly stacked so as to be able to more quickly calculate the size of a bet.

On the flip side of the coin, it's somewhat true that a player who stacks his chips carelessly is likely to be loose, inexperienced, or very nervous.

Asking naïve questions, or unfamiliar with procedure. Sometimes it will be obvious that a player is inexperienced based on how clumsily he handles his chips or cards, or on a naïve question he asks about posting blinds in hold'em or the double-bet with a pair showing on Fourth Street in seven-card stud. Occasionally a tricky player will try to act inexperienced by asking dumb questions or otherwise acting as if he just came in off the farm, but usually they'll do so in a suspiciously broad manner. The best thing about players like this is that they're usually not very good—they're too busy concentrating on gimmicks and angle-shooting to play a solid game.

You do need to watch out, however, for a player who plays very few hands, is aggressive when playing them, and otherwise seems knowledgeable—but is strangely awkward just the same. This may be someone who's learned hold'em by clicking a mouse in the privacy of his or her home, but hasn't quite gotten used to the feel of real cards and chips. In other words—an Internet kid.

Your main advantage against mouse-clickers is that they're likely to give off many more tells than usual, at least until they gain composure. I recently played a limit hold'em game at Foxwoods Casino sitting next to a serious young man who literally lost his voice on being dealt Aces and then flopping a set head-up. Sure enough, he later told me he was an Internet veteran playing his very first casino sit. His hand-reading skills had been nicely developed within the sterile confines of online play, so it was no surprise that he came away with a win.

Also remember that just because a player handles his cards and chips as well as Gus Hansen (or better—if you watch the World Poker Tour you'll see that Gus tends to fumble his chip-riffling when he's thinking hard), it doesn't mean he plays well. Most fish graduate to chip-riffling after several years of draining away their bankrolls; it comes with fish territory.

Expressing luck-oriented beliefs. If you discover a player enjoys talking about hot and cold seats, lucky versus unlucky dealers, and how the cards are running today, don't dismiss him as a moron and leave it at that. Instead, listen to see if he's just amusing himself or really believes in this stuff. If it turns out he's serious, bless the gods of luck that brought him to your table. Since he doesn't understand probability, he'll almost certainly be horribly loose on all streets, chasing with all sorts of hands a good player would throw away. Even so, you'll want to keep close tabs on his betting patterns, which will be more erratic than the orbit of Pluto. Bet your fair hands for value against him, and be careful if he plays back unexpectedly on later streets—he'll draw out on you far more than you'll draw out on him.

By the way, it's interesting to note that quite a few big-name players are superstitious themselves. These superstitions tend not to involve probabilities at the table; instead they revolve around the kinds of totems and taboos that obsess baseball players and other big-time athletes—lucky shirts or hats, jewelry, rituals before playing, etc.

Watching TV, reading at the table. A player who consistently keeps his or her eyes on the casino TV is betraying either a lack of concentration at the moment or, more likely, a lack of poker education: if the first rule of poker is to learn a sound fundamental game, the second is to observe your opponents. Very likely such an opponent will be a loose-passive player; loose-aggressive players tend to watch the action more.

A player who's got his eyes glued to a book or a magazine is committing a similar sin, but with this difference: he's more likely than the TV watcher to know a bit about poker. What he's doing is keeping himself from getting bored while he waits for a strong starting hand to play. He's likely to be unimaginative, the sort of player who stopped learning about the game once he decided that "tight is right."

If he enters a pot, therefore, it'll be with extra-good starting cards. He'll be reluctant to fold those good cards, too, so don't bother bluffing against him. Do, however, bet your strong hands all the way, as he's more likely to pay you off with something like an unimproved overpair. If you're seated to his right, think about raising more often than you otherwise might if you're opening in late position or if he's in the blinds because a steal attempt is more likely to be successful—he's unimaginative, remember, so it's going to take him longer than usual to adjust.

Drinking alcohol at the table. Someone who's sipping a beer or a Bloody Mary is usually going to pay in chips for the privilege, whether or not the drinks themselves are free. Even if the player isn't actually intoxicated, his casual attitude indicates he's more interested in having fun than in winning. Again, there are rare exceptions: Men "the Master" Nguyen drinks Corona beer while playing tournaments; he claims it calms his nerves and doesn't hurt his play otherwise. It's unlikely you're going to run into someone of Nguyen's caliber at your local casino, but you might run into a player who's having a drink or two yet still plays a pretty tough game. Again, keep your assumptions on a leash until they're confirmed or denied.

A player who's not just drinking, but actually drunk, is more likely to call in all circumstances. Forget about bluffing and start doing more value-betting.

Gambling on the side. If a player discloses through conversation that he likes to shoot craps, or if you notice he's writing out Keno tickets or betting the horses in between poker hands, you know he likes to gamble; now you've got to watch closely to see what form this urge takes when he's got cards in his hands.

At the low limits, most gambling addicts tend to crave action more than edge; they'll probably play a loose game, possibly with a little extra aggression. But if you play the higher limits, watch out: throughout poker history, many of the very best high-stakes players have been action junkies. Such players will win and lose large amounts betting on sports, golf matches, and propositions that by-the-book players would reject as insane. For example, two top players sitting next to each other in a cash game may set up a running side bet on whether the next upcard dealt will be red or black. Unless you're a top player yourself, now would be a good time to find another table.

Posture. Some poker authorities will tell you that a player leaning back in the chair, relaxed yet confident, is waiting for a good hand; therefore you're advised not to tangle with him unless you've got a solid hand yourself. My response to this is, you'll know he's waiting for a good hand by the fact he's folding so much. A player with a tight mentality may lean back in the seat or may sit forward; he or she may appear tense or relaxed. None of this is important.

Posture does become important once you've sat at the table long enough to notice who's winning and who's losing. Losers who adopt a slump-shouldered, beaten pose are unlikely to be playing their best; their eyes will often be somewhat glazed, and they'll tend to grab at each fresh set of starting cards like a drowning man at a life preserver. Losers who have the self-control to maintain an upright, unfazed posture, on the other hand, are much more likely to be dangerous opponents.

Other Cues Exhibited by Bad Players

Romantic gabbers. Players who talk a lot about a hand afterward usually aren't very good. The best players rarely talk much. If you sit down at a no-limit table and it seems like four or five guys are constantly jawing happily at each other about the last hand they played together, this is probably a good table. Such players tend to be young and inexperienced, with most of their supposed poker knowledge coming from television; their main interest is in self-dramatization, not winning. Occasionally you'll see this sort of grandstanding in a limit game as well; this usually indicates someone who has watched no-limit on TV but played little poker of any kind.

Beaten card flashers. Players who show an opponent one or both of their hole cards as they fold are trying to save face. ("See what a big lay-down I made for you?") They're either embarrassed at having gotten caught with a substandard hand, or highly risk-averse. And that means they're probably too loose in the early going, and too tight and passive on later streets. Such traits make them a natural target, especially in no-limit.

To be more specific, a player who displays these kinds of self-defeating mannerisms may well talk himself into folding if you bluff him in a spot where you've got absolutely nothing, but have a read that he doesn't hold much either. It might even work if he holds a real hand like a big overpair, but the board comes very scary, allowing you to represent the holding he most fears. In the face of your big bet or raise, he'll start verbalizing out loud, and what will emerge is his belief that you hold exactly that hand that will crack him. Your silence confirms his dread, and so he folds out of what he imagines to be self-preservation.

Following Up First Impressions

Of course, all of this supposes that you're correcting your first impressions with a steady trickle of observations of hands shown down, betting patterns, and so on. If, for example, you saw that a card flasher sought to save face whenever he got caught on a steal, but was otherwise a total calling station, you'd never bluff him as just described.

What sort of things should you be looking for with betting patterns? Here's a short checklist to give you ideas:

♣ How many hands does he play? How often is he raising versus limping?

♣ What hands will he limp in with and at what positions? Raise with? Call a raise with?

♣ How does he play big hands? Is he a habitual slow-player, or does he play big hands fast?

♣ Is he keeping track of the pot? Does he care about pot odds and implied odds, or not?

♣ Is he a calling station? Does he bet for value on the end, or check? Does he like to check-raise a lot?

♣ Does he adjust his play for different situations? Does he play differently against different players? If so, can you follow his thinking? Does it make sense to you?

Once you've got a line on a player's hand values and betting patterns, you can start to look for tells—now you've got a context into which to put them. With this as our background, we're ready to discuss generic tells in detail, starting in the next chapter.

CHAPTER 4

GENERIC TELLS IN LIMIT POKER

You've been leading the betting in a seven-card stud hand with split Aces that improve to Aces up. Your remaining opponent seems to be chasing with what you judge to be two medium pair. When he gets his river card, he takes a peek at it, then pushes it away and waits impassively for you to act. Well, you've *got* to value-bet your hand here, right? But even as your chips hit the felt, he's pulling his hole cards back for a second look. This confuses you. It confuses you even more when he puts forth double your number of chips, indicating a raise.

What in the world is going on?

This is only one of more than two dozen generic tells we'll examine in this chapter. Nearly all of these tells relate to limit hold'em and limit seven-card stud—we're saving no-limit hold'em for the next chapter. I'm also including a few tells for Omaha eight-or-better and stud high-low, but only a few: tells are of somewhat less value in these games, given the peculiar nature of high-low poker.

One other caution: remember that these tells are rendered slightly artificial by the need to present them as a single example in each case. In real life, tells vary in their details, all depending on the player and the situation. It's like bird-watching: learn the markers for a given bird, and you can recognize it in the dark, from behind, as a juvenile specimen, and so on—it's always the same bird, even though an unskilled observer might think it was three or four different ones.

Telegraphs with Starting Cards

A telegraph is a special kind of tell, one that indicates how a player feels about his starting cards *before* the action gets to him. Naïve players are more likely to display telegraphs than experienced players, for the simple reason that they're more eager to see if they've gotten lucky. There's an exception to this in hold'em: even experienced players are likely to take a quick look when they're in the blinds. We'll talk more about this whole subject of when to look in chapter 8, "Avoiding Tells Yourself."

Tell: Freezing up before raising.

Example: You're in middle position in a limit hold'em game. As several early players fold, you notice in your peripheral vision that the player to your immediate left is sneaking a look at her hole cards. Now she pushes the cards slightly away from her—but not too far—and withdraws her hands to the rail, going completely motionless.

Explanation: She's picked up a good hand, very likely a raising hand, and her instinct is to avoid drawing attention to herself. So she freezes. You'll need to see a player do this more than once to establish the link between the telegraph and the raise, but once that link is made, the tell is highly reliable.

What to do: If you don't find you've got a raising hand yourself, fold. If you get lucky and find a huge hand like pocket Aces or Kings, limp with the intention of reraising.

Tell: Great disdain to play these cards.

Example: Same theme as the preceding, but now we're playing seven-card stud. And this time, rather than freeze up, the player in question rests his chin on his hand as if bored, looks away from the action, or in some other way attempts to suggest with body language that he's totally uninterested in the great hole cards he just saw.

Explanation: This tell is just as reliable as the freeze tell, but is often easier to detect because of the exaggerated acting.

What to do: As in the hold'em example, once you can reliably link this tell up with the intent to raise, play your own cards accordingly.

Tell: Grabbing chips.

Example: Seven-card stud: you're thinking of limping a small three-flush. But then the player across the table from you with an Ace doorcard looks at his hole cards and immediately picks up chips from his stack.

Explanation: He's got split Aces. This tell is surprisingly common among naïve stud players and very reliable in that setting. For whatever reason, it's much rarer in hold'em.

What to do: Same as with other telegraphs. In this case you'd probably want to fold your small three-flush.

Tell: Premature folding.

Example: A player in either hold'em or stud peeks at her hole cards. Then she shifts her grip so that she can more easily flick them in the muck when it's her turn to act. Meanwhile her attention wanders away to the TV set, or the waitress, or anything but the action.

Explanation: In one sense, you can understand why a player might behave like this; if she's going to fold anyway, why worry about concealing it? The problem is, she's still disclosing information about her approach to the game. For one thing, she's more likely to be passive than aggressive—aggressive players like to steal when they can, and this tell would ruin it for them. For another, such laxness is a good indicator she's likely to be highly readable in other ways.

What to do: Be aware of the implications I've described and adjust accordingly. In addition, if one or more players with this tell happen to be seated to your left, stay alert for opportunities to steal with weaker cards than usual.

Tell: Counting players for a draw.

Example: In hold'em, several early-position players limp in. It gets to a player who you judge to be at least moderately tight before the flop; he looks at his hole cards, then looks up and glances around the table. Either his head bobs slightly or his lips move—either way, it's clear he's counting how many players are already in or seem likely to come in. He nods to himself, satisfied, and puts forth enough chips to limp.

Explanation: He's got a drawing hand—maybe suited connectors or a suited QT or similar. It's probably not suited trash or a junk hand like K3 because a player who cares enough to count his potential pot odds usually won't play those kinds of hands. Nor is it an offsuit big-card hand like KJ, because he wouldn't consider that a drawing hand and therefore wouldn't count how many players were in.

What to do: If he appears to like the flop, you'll have at least a small head start at guessing how his hand fits it.

Tells on Later Streets

Tell: Glancing at chips.

Example: From hold'em: you're in late position in a three-way unraised pot. The flop comes with a possible draw, giving you a weak but passable top pair. The big blind hesitates, glances at his chips, then taps the table. The middle position player checks also; now it's to you.

Explanation: The big blind wanted to bet—hence the glance at his chips—but held up after thinking about it. This is a highly reliable tell in all games. Sometimes the player will actually go so far as to reach for his chips before pulling his hand away.

What to do: A lot depends on the situation here. Maybe the big blind has a draw and thought about betting it; or maybe he's flopped something like bottom two pair that he'd like to protect with a check-raise. In the former situation you'd want to bet your weak top pair; in the latter, you wouldn't. In this case, the pot is small, so that's another factor affecting your decision.

Tell: Looking away.

Example: A loose-aggressive hold'em player open-raises in middle position. He could have nearly anything in this spot, from a small pocket pair to AK. You as dealer reraise with TT and get head-up. The flop comes J♦3♣7♣, and immediately your opponent looks off into space. Then he looks back at the flop, assumes a sour expression, and checks to you.

Explanation: He's flopped good—so good he instinctively tried to conceal it by looking away from the action. In this example his look away is brief, but with a naïve player it might be more extended or elaborate. With some players it might be just the eyes that flick away for a moment, then back again. In seven-card stud, this same tell can occur when a player gets an up-card that helps him.

Is this tell restricted to limit poker—or, for that matter, to unsophisticated players? The answer in both cases is no. Check out the Bicycle Casino's *Legends of Poker* final table, available on DVD as part of Season Two of the World Poker Tour; in particular, watch for poker legend T. J. Cloutier's sudden stare into space in a head-up hand versus the less-experienced Paul Phillips. Cloutier is holding AJ here in a reraised pot, and he's spiked a Jack on the flop. His recovery is instantaneous, but it's interesting that (a) as experienced a player as Cloutier can't help himself here, and (b) his weaker opponent completely fails to pick up on it.

What to do: In our example from limit hold'em, unless your opponent salivates at the sight of a draw and has flopped a Club draw here, your pocket Tens are probably no good. But say you hold JJ rather than TT and have flopped top set: now you welcome action and hope his tell indicates he's flopped something like a set of Sevens. As always, you should seek to supplement this tell with knowledge of his betting patterns: have you seen him check-raise with a draw out of position? Does he prefer to fastplay or slowplay a big hand like a set?

Tell: Too quick to be true.

Example: In hold'em, you raise in late position with AK and get one caller, a loose, tricky player in the big blind. From watching him, you know he tends to chase with weak hands and likes to bluff. The flop comes King-high rainbow, giving you top pair. He checks, you bet, he calls. The turn puts a second Spade on board, but otherwise appears unthreatening; again he check-calls. Now the river brings another baby Spade, making possible a backdoor flush. Immediately when the Spade hits, your opponent sits up straight, looks you in the eye, and bets, sweeping his hand forward to lay down the chips.

Explanation: You're somewhat handicapped by the fact that this opponent is tricky to begin with; it's remotely possible that he *did* hit a backdoor flush and is deliberately exaggerating his movements in hopes you'll think he's acting when he's not. Far more likely, however, is that he's got a terrible hand like middle pair or a busted gutshot straight draw.

What gives him away is his instant response when the scary flush card hits. Most players who actually *do* backdoor a flush here will spend at least a few seconds considering whether they should bet or try for a check-raise. And the exaggerated betting motion probably means he's weak here but wants to appear strong, exactly in line with the classic Mike Caro maxim about actors (see p. 20).

As with all tells that might indicate a bluff, it also matters whether you're head-up or multiway. In limit poker, even a tricky player would be much less likely to attempt a bluff with several players in the pot.

Now guess which big-name player has displayed this tell in a recent tournament. Hey, it's T. J. Cloutier again, in the very same hand against Paul Phillips where he did the look-away tell! A Club comes on the turn, and T.J. immediately sits up, glares at Phillips, and bangs out a $200,000 bet, representing a made flush instead of the lousy pair of Jacks he really holds. The acting job so impresses Phillips that he folds the best hand *and* the best draw—pocket Queens with the Queen of Clubs. If T.J. had really hit that flush, his reaction and his motions would have been more deliberate.

What to do: If you read this tell right, folding isn't an option if you're head-up. Whether you just call or raise depends on whether you yourself have a real hand. If all you've got is a busted draw yourself, this would be a good time for a raise. Admittedly, that calls for not only a good read but quick, creative thinking.

Tell: Betting out of turn.

Example: In seven-card stud, a player with a Ten as his doorcard has just been calling along in a three-way pot versus one player who appears to be on a small flush draw and another player who's driving the action with what appears to be split Aces. On Sixth Street the first player is dealt a Jack; the other two players get blanks. The showing Ace is still high, but before that player can do anything, the player who just got the Jack bets. Then he apologizes and pulls his bet back.

Explanation: Almost certainly this player has improved his hand; the question is to what. Would he bet out of turn with two pair? Not likely. You'd have to give strong consideration to his having caught a third Jack to go with the pocket Jacks he was calling along with, especially if his body language betrays excitement in some other way.

In a variation, the player checks out of turn rather than bets out of turn. It's not as easy to interpret as the bet out of turn, but could mean he wanted to check-raise and got too eager.

What to do: In our example, the player with the Aces should consider checking here. However, a lot depends on how confident he is in his reads. Strong stud players develop an almost uncanny feel for what opponents hold, based on dead cards, betting patterns, and tells.

Tell: Yapping at the bettor.

Example: You're head-up in a limit hold'em game, having raised preflop in early position and gotten called by only the cutoff. You flop top pair on a ragged board and bet; he calls, grumbling. The turn comes a blank, and now before you can bet, he starts jawing at you. "Do you really want to bet that? I'd be careful! Watch out!"

Explanation: He's got some kind of weak hand that he'd like to see another card with—maybe middle pair, maybe a gutshot draw. By talking, he hopes to intimidate you into checking to him. This sort of tell occurs in all games and is highly reliable.

What to do: As Caro advises, when confronted with a clear-cut case of acting, you're usually safe in doing the opposite of what the actor wants. In this case, go ahead and bet.

Tell: Grabbing chips to intimidate.

Example: The exact same situation as just described, only this time the player doesn't jaw at you, he just grabs a bunch of chips from his stack and holds them so you can see them.

Explanation: Again he doesn't want you to bet. He's trying to make it clear that he's going to call if you do so, hoping this will slow you down. In some cases he may hold his chips as if threatening to raise; this is usually an even bigger sign of weakness.

What to do: Once again, do the opposite of what the actor wants and bet your hand.

Tell: Trembling hands.

Example: In hold'em, you've put in the third raise in the small blind with A♦A♥; six players are in for what is already a monster pot. The flop comes Q♦J♦9♦, giving you an overpair with an Ace-high flush draw. The flop is bet and raised twice; four players remain to see the turn. It comes the King of Diamonds, giving you the flush, but also making a straight flush possible if someone holds the Ten of Diamonds by itself. You bet out. One player calls and the next, who until now was just calling along, starts picking up chips to raise. That's when you notice his hand is trembling violently.

Explanation: This tell is useless for players whose hands normally tremble—including some younger players as well as older players. But for anyone whose hands *don't* normally tremble, it's a huge tell in all forms of poker.

What to do: Your Ace-high flush is no good; your opponent has made the straight flush. Players who've never seen this tell may have a hard time believing it, but yes, it's that powerful an indicator. Moreover, it can't be faked with any degree of realism. But what if he's misread his hand? Go ahead and call down if you feel you must, but avoid putting in any raises. It helps to support your read that the straight flush is relatively easy to make here, requiring only one key card, not two.

Tell: Did I just pair my other card?

Example: In seven-card stud, you call with a big flush start, AKQ of Diamonds, against a player you suspect holds split Jacks. On Fourth Street you catch a blank, while he catches a Four. Immediately he checks his down cards.

Explanation: He's got some little card to go with his Jacks, but doesn't remember what it is, so he has to check. This tell is common to weak players, who have a hard time remembering their cards, but you won't find it in stronger players.

What to do: If you had any doubts, this tell rules out your opponent having started out rolled up or having just made trip Fours. At best he's made Jacks up here, so play accordingly.

Tell: Oops, check for suits.

Example: A loose, low-limit hold'em game. The flop comes all Hearts and two of your opponents immediately check their hole cards.

Explanation: Weak players who limp offsuit hands often can't be bothered to keep track of the suits. An interesting wrinkle occurs when it's the preflop raiser who checks for suit like this—if he's holding a big pair or two big cards, he's either got a big flush draw or no flush draw at all.

What to do: In this example, you can rule out either of these players holding two Hearts. If it's the preflop raiser who's double-checking, watch to see if his actions are consistent with having either a strong draw or an endangered made hand, rather than anything in the middle.

Tell: Let me just straighten out these great cards.

Example: In seven-card stud, you've got Kings up in a multiway pot against several loose players. One player in particular starts with a Ten as her upcard, gets a Queen on Fourth Street, and a Nine on Fifth. When she's dealt the Queen, she carefully lines it up with her other upcard; when she gets the Nine, she does the same thing.

Explanation: Many stud players at all levels will adjust their upcards during the course of a deal; what you want to watch for is the weak player who only does it with hands she really likes. After all, it's hardly worth arranging cards you're planning to toss into the muck. In this case, look for the player to have either a made straight or an open-ended straight draw.

What to do: If you've verified this is a valid tell for this player, you may want to check your Kings up here and see what she does. The fact that you have two Kings may be cutting off some of her straight outs—that is, if she hasn't made the straight already.

Tell: Let's gamble!

Example: In hold'em, it's four limpers and the small blind to you in the big blind; you check with J9. The flop comes Nine-high, but given the looseness of the game, you're reluctant to bet your top pair, mediocre kicker. At any rate it's checked around. The turn pairs the bottom card on the board, and this time the small blind says, "Ah, c'mon, fellows, let's get some money in this pot," and bets.

Explanation: This fellow's a born actor. Although you might want to believe he's betting this scary turn card as a bluff, the verbal tell indicates he's got the trips. This tell occurs mostly with weak and intermediate players—although some strong players may display traces of it themselves, in the form of talking excessively when they hit a big hand. It's always highly reliable once spotted. A common variant is the player who says, "Hey guys, let's gamble!" or "I feel like gambling here"—believe him at your peril.

What to do: Fold your lousy top pair and save yourself the money.

Tell: Pretend-folding to induce a bet.

Example: You raise with AQ on the button in hold'em, and only the big blind calls. The board comes KQ3 rainbow, and he check-calls your bet there. The turn comes a blank, he checks, and you figure you might as well bet, though you don't know if you're ahead or behind. On the river, he again checks; you reach for your chips to bet, but hesitate. He sees the hesitation and gestures with his cards as if about to muck them.

Explanation: He's trying to get you to bet so he can check-raise with whatever hand he's been trapping with. Most likely he can beat a pair of Kings, let alone Queens.

What to do: You've got to check here. This tell is more of a blatant attempt at manipulation than anything else. Because it doesn't occur very often, it may catch you by surprise.

Tell: Don't mind me and my monster.

Example: A hold'em game. With two limpers to you, you raise in late position with AK; the small blind calls, as do the limpers. The flop comes AJ4; only the small blind and one limper call your bet. The turn brings a Five, which under the circumstances doesn't seem too threatening; the small blind checks with a blank look on her face. She seems to be staring into space, rather than at the flop or any of the players.

Explanation: You've got to know this player's baseline behavior. If normally she'd be following the action and now she isn't, you're in trouble. The five might have given her two pair, but more likely (given her attempt to disappear), it gave her a wheel. This is a big tell in all games, with many individual variations. In all cases the player tries to appear as innocuous and uninterested as possible, so as to avoid inhibiting anyone from betting. Note that if she had position and was the last player to act rather than the first, she'd have less interest in slowplaying.

What to do: Given that it's limit, you won't be throwing your hand away—but you've got to check here, and do no more than call on the river if she bets there.

Tell: A shaking leg.

Example: A hold'em game. During a hand you're out of, you notice that a solid, rather impassive opponent is moving his head up and down ever so slightly in a very fast rhythm—almost like a bobble-head doll. Glancing under the table, you realize the movement is actually being caused by his rapidly bouncing leg. You realize too that the turn card has put a possible flush on board, and the leg-bouncer has seized the initiative by betting out into his opponent. After a pause, his opponent reluctantly folds.

You watch this guy closely for the next 20 minutes, during which he wins a couple of pots with solid hands such as top pair and two pair; the leg remains motionless. Then you flop top pair in a hand against him. It's checked to you, two other players fold, he calls, and the two of you see the turn head up. An overcard comes, simultaneously putting a two-flush on board, and he bets out. Very scary. You're considering what to do when you notice his head bobbing—it's that leg thing again!

Explanation: Given that you've seen him make a couple of legitimate hands without bouncing, it's a good guess that he gets nervous like this only when bluffing or semi-bluffing. It's important to make the correlation here between the tell and the betting pattern, because quite a few players have the *opposite* tendency—they'll bounce a leg or otherwise display agitation only when they hit a big hand, not when bluffing. So make sure you know your player.

What to do: Seeing the two-flush, you decide to raise here based on your tell; if he's on a draw as you suspect, you want to extract the maximum from him. He calls, but check-folds to your river bet when no third flush card comes. You don't get to see his cards, of course, but now you've got even more reason to suspect his leg tell occurs only when he's semi-bluffing.

Your turn raise has other advantages, too. Say the river brings the third flush card: if in fact he's made the flush, he may well check here, believing your raise on the turn makes it highly likely you'll bet the river. Instead, you'll check behind, foiling his play. Again you have the tell to thank for minimizing your potential loss.

Tell: Suddenly alert.

Example: In seven-card stud, you're playing a big four-flush against a mediocre opponent who likely started with a medium pair. You make your flush on Fifth Street while your opponent makes an open small pair; she checks, you bet, she calls. Both of you catch blanks on Sixth; you bet and again she tiredly calls, not even bothering to look up. On Seventh, you're already counting the pot, but as she examines her river card she suddenly straightens up and looks you in the eye. But then she taps the felt, indicating a check.

Explanation: She's been trailing along with two pair; her sudden interest is because she's filled up. Even an average player will figure you've been betting a made flush up to this point. The only reason she's checking here is so she can check-raise.

What to do: If your hand is as transparent as in this instance, you must check behind. Only if your real hand is stronger than your opponent suspects can you think about opening up the action.

Tell: Missing a draw and slumping.

Example: Whether in seven-card stud or hold'em, an opponent who may be on a draw sees the river card and his shoulders slump ever-so-slightly, just for a moment.

Explanation: He's missed his draw. If he's head-up with you, his problem now is figuring out whether he should attempt a bluff. The only exception here might be if he held a strong made hand already, but was drawing at a monster and is disappointed he missed it.

What to do: If you spot the slump and read it as real, you'll generally want to bet if you're head-up. Say you were on a draw and missed yourself: a bet here might allow you to pick up the pot. Likewise, if you hold a decent hand, you may as well value-bet it. An advantage of betting and not getting called by the busted draw is that you don't have to show your hand down—and since poker is a game of information, you usually want to show down as few hands as possible. (The exception is if you're trying to manipulate your opponent—but most of us aren't as good at manipulation as we might like to believe.)

Tell: Disgusted enough to call.

Example: You're in a hold'em pot that started multi-way, but has become head-up. Your opponent was driving the betting all the way on a fairly scary board—a King and a Jack flopped, and a Queen came on the turn. The river comes a Four; he grimaces, then checks to you. You started with a medium flush draw, which didn't come in, but the Queen on the turn paired your high card. Should you bet?

Explanation: Many players will routinely check their good but not super-strong hands on the river; this fellow is likely one of them. There's a good chance he's disgusted only because he didn't make a big hand such as a Broadway straight, not because he doesn't have any hand at all. Remember, he's letting you *see* the disgust, which he wouldn't want to do if he was truly weak; in such a case, he'd try to appear stronger than he was—maybe even taking another bet at the pot in hopes you'd fold exactly the sort of hand you in fact have.

What to do: Check your second pair and expect him to show down a King to match the one on the board.

Tell: Shuffling on a draw.

Example: In seven-card stud, you raise on Third Street with split Queens and get two callers. One has a Ten showing, and you know she's prone to chasing with under-pairs; the other has a Seven showing, but he's so loose it's hard to put him on a specific hand. You make Queens up on Fifth Street and continue to lead the betting there and on Sixth Street. The player with the Ten doorcard hasn't paired her board yet, so you figure she's unimproved; meanwhile the Seven doorcard has accumulated a Four, Eight, Jack, and King of various suits. You notice that when he gets his river card, he doesn't look at it, but shuffles it with his other cards as he waits for the betting to get to him.

Explanation: This is an old draw poker tell, but also occurs in stud: players who like to chase draws often like to keep themselves in suspense as long as they can; the shuffling on the river helps them do this. Even when they do look, they tend to squeeze their cards out slowly, once again maximizing the suspense. An additional clue is if they then glance back and forth between their hole cards and their upcards, looking to see if the straight might somehow be there.

In hold'em, some players also have a habit of shuffling their down cards. In this case, however, it's usually just an expression of tension.

What to do: Again, everything is situational. If the player with the Ten doorcard is looking like she never improved her one pair and won't call a bet here, a check might be better: the third player won't call you if he missed his small straight draw, but will raise you if he made it. If, however, you think the Tens *will* call a bet, now you have to take your chances and try to get value for your hand; most of the time he'll have missed his straight, and those times he's hit you can usually safely fold to his raise—especially if the Tens have already called in front of him, minimizing the chances he's bluffing.

Tell: Is that monster still under the bed?

Example: This is from the introduction to this chapter —that seven-card stud hand where you're betting your Aces up against one caller with what you believe to be two medium pair. You go ahead and value-bet your hand on the river, and he double-checks his hole cards before raising you.

Explanation: He's caught a great river card for a medium full house. But he's not sure you'll call his raise, so the sneaky side of his soul whispers in his ear that he should pretend to double-check his cards. Logically it doesn't quite make sense, but it's confusing enough that most players with the Aces up will call here just to see what's going on.

What to do: If it's a small pot and you know your player, you can fold here. If you *don't* know your player, you need to call to gain information for future hands.

Tell: Talking you into calling.

Example: Head-up in a hold'em game. The pot was unraised preflop, and you've been calling along on the flop and turn with top pair, medium kicker; the river comes a seeming blank, but your opponent bets out again regardless. As he does, he smiles at you and issues what might be either a taunt or kindly advice, depending on how you look at it. "You can't call here," he says. "Fold and save your chips."

Explanation: No matter what the tone of voice or exact phrasing, his underlying intent is exactly the opposite of his words: he's trying to goad you into calling.

Interestingly, you can find this tell online, too. Recently, I was playing in an online hold'em game with a player who'd been making liberal use of the chat feature to lambaste other players for things like sucking out with weak draws. Soon I found myself head-up with this guy on the river, holding no better than middle pair on a ragged board. I had a feeling I was beat, but I was prepared to make a crying call—that is, until my opponent typed in the following chat message: "Come on and call, you piece of crap." That was all I needed to click Fold instead. Of course, the pot was small here, helping my decision, but the tell was the clincher.

What to do: In virtually every case, unless your hand has hidden strength, follow Caro's law and do the opposite of what your opponent really wants: go ahead and fold.

Tells in High-Low Split Games

This is going to be a relatively short section—for the simple reason that in high-low games, it's even more important than in high-only games to concentrate most of your attention on reading hands through betting patterns and boards. That doesn't mean that tells are completely nonexistent, though. Following are some things to look for.

Omaha High-Low

Unless played short-handed, limit Omaha high-low is a game that rewards playing to the nuts more than it does tricky plays or intuitive reads. Bluffing becomes nearly impossible, so tells related to bluffing likewise nearly disappear. Still, there *are* tells in this game—in particular, the following two occur often enough that it pays to watch for them especially.

Tell: Weak hands require lots of thought.

Example: A short-handed Omaha game, with only six players. In late position in a family pot you limp A35T, a very weak hand; the flop comes 479, giving you a draw to the second nut low. There's one bet and four players call, including you. The turn is the King of Diamonds, putting a two-flush in Diamonds on board; again there's only one bet, which all four players call. The river brings an eight of Clubs, making you what is likely the winning low, given the lack of action. There's a bet and a call to you; two players will be acting after you. One thing you've noticed: the action on all streets so far has been painfully slow; no one has been making any snap decisions.

Explanation: The lack of a raise on any street so far is a pretty big indicator that your second-nut low is likely a monster this time around. And then there's the tell itself: namely, how long everyone's taking to make their decisions.

In Omaha, strong hands require relatively little thought, while weak hands require lots and lots of it—players have to struggle to figure out where they are and whether they have any draw at all. There are usually some tricky opponents who will limp an A2 prior to the flop and slowplay it for one or two streets, or even to the river—but they'd have checked quickly when it was their turn, not gone into the tank. Even someone who held the same second-best low as you do, an A3, wouldn't require very much time to make a decision here—so you're probably not going to get quartered, either.

What to do: Since you can't depend on the two players behind you to call the initial bet, you should almost certainly raise and collect from the two players already in.

Tell: Scary card conceals the nuts.

Example: Let's use the same example hand as the preceding, but this time the player seated to your right is checking and calling with only a slight hesitation whenever it's her turn to act. As in the previous example, the flop comes rainbow, and the turn brings a two-flush in Diamonds; not much action on either street. This time, however, the river comes an Eight of Diamonds, making a flush possible—and suddenly the player you've been watching springs to life, raising the bet instead of just calling.

Explanation: Actually, there are two tells here—the first one being that this player didn't hesitate very long when it was her turn to act. That means she likely had a real draw of some kind. If you think back, her call on the flop was as quick as her call on the turn, so that seems to weigh against a backdoor flush draw. What's she got, then? Most likely the nut low, which she was slowplaying all along. The scary Diamond has given her the perfect excuse to raise here and represent the high. That unexpected raise is the second tell.

What to do: A tough decision, but remember that the pot is fairly small given the lack of action, and you can only win half in this case no matter what. A fold will be easier if you've been tracking this player's betting patterns and know she tends to slowplay her nut hands, especially nut lows.

Stud High-Low

Stud high-low is another game where loose players often chase half the pot with bad draws; as in Omaha high-low, knowledge of betting patterns is more important than tells per se. For example, knowing that a player is a loose-passive calling station will help you in every hand you play against him, where a tell might help you only occasionally.

Again, that doesn't mean there aren't any tells worth looking for. In terms of generic tells, you can find the same telegraphs in high-low stud as you do in high-only stud. And you'll also encounter such generic tells as trembling hands with a monster, shuffling on a draw, and so on.

Declare High-Low

Stud high-low with a declare is never played in casinos, but it's common in home games. When cards no longer speak, tells pick up value as players are forced into harder decisions with weak hands. Even in a loose game, the use of tells plus superior card-reading ability can allow a strong player to steal more than his share of pots. Tells to look for include:

- ♣ Involuntary signs of confidence, such as a bored or mechanical voice when betting a lock hand.
- ♣ Extra-long delays when making a decision (but be careful the player isn't weighing whether to declare both ways).
- ♣ Eyes darting around the various boards as the player tries to decide whether high or low represents his best chances for an escape.
- ♣ Tells from actors with strong hands who want to appear weak—for example, double-checking hole cards and then calling.

Following is an example that illustrates the niceties involved in reading high-low stud tells, as opposed to high-only.

Tell: Disappointed but still calling.

Example: You're playing high-low stud declare in a $1–$5 spread-limit home game; the convention in this game is that the best low is a 6–4, not a wheel. Four of you get past Third Street, with one player jamming there with an Ace showing; he catches a Jack on Fourth, but again raises. He's normally a very loose-passive player, so all this jamming makes you wonder whether he's got something more than just split Aces.

On Fifth Street he catches an Eight and calls along rather than raise; on Sixth, he catches a Nine and sighs loudly. The river card sees him shake his head in what seems like genuine disappointment. Meanwhile, your own Six-low start has busted out, and you've got no high and only a Ten low. This guy looks to be your only competition for the low side of the pot; should you try to force him out after the declare by betting or raising the maximum?

Explanation: This player is most likely disappointed because he held an ultra-strong low hand—possibly an A23 or something similar—that didn't improve to a wheel or a nut low as he hoped it would. Given his board and the fact that he's not bothering to conceal his disappointment, there's a good chance he's got something like an Eight low that he'll feel obliged to call with.

What to do: Save your money. Go ahead and declare low—but if there's any significant action, be prepared to fold rather than tilt after this particular windmill.

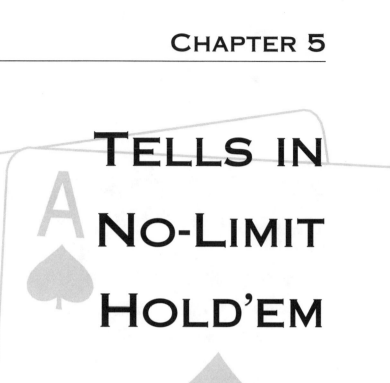

CHAPTER 5

TELLS IN NO-LIMIT HOLD'EM

All of the tells for limit hold'em can be found in no-limit as well—but there are a handful that occur more frequently in no-limit, often with a twist. Beyond that, no-limit features some unique tells that *never* appear in limit. Here's a quick example from my own experience to give you the idea.

I'm not a tournament player—I've played in fewer than a half-dozen no-limit tournaments in my life, all of them small, club-sponsored affairs. One of these I actually won, but I remember it less for that, and more for the following little drama that took place on the second-to-last table.

We were down to four players at the table, and I was pretty short stacked—about eight times the big blind. It seemed highly fortunate when it was folded to me on the button, and I looked down to find pocket Sevens. Without too much thought I raised a little more than half my stack—probably the wrong move, but like I said, I'm not a tournament player. The small blind folded, and the big blind went ballistic.

"That was a string raise!" he spat at the dealer. "He put out half his chips, then the other half! He can't do that!"

I'd played with this fellow in some $4/$8 limit games, and I knew from experience that he was a very bad limit player, too impatient and too tricky for his own good. Even so he had me well-covered here, and I didn't understand what his problem was. The jabbering and the fussing didn't seem quite real.

The dealer reassured him that my raise had been legitimate. The big blind began playing with his chips, pushing stacks forward, then pulling them back. He was still complaining loudly, but he was eyeing my stack, too. The small blind had been watching in amusement; he leaned toward me as if to tell me something, but then pulled back.

That's when I realized what the play-acting was all about. "If you want to put me all-in," I told the big blind, "go ahead. I'm too short-stacked not to call."

"Screw you," he said, but relief shone on his face; he'd been deathly afraid I'd fold and waste his big hand. "Aces," the small blind whispered as I pushed my remaining chips forward, and of course, that's exactly what the big blind flipped over. The end of this story is that I rivered a Seven-high straight, putting the actor on tilt; he busted out a few hands later, while I went on to glory. Now *that* was a tell—one of the crazier ones I've ever witnessed.

When the Betting Gets Big

I've seen the big-hand stall many times since, and I'm sure I'll keep seeing it as long as I play no-limit poker. You're probably familiar with it yourself. It won't fool the pros, but it does have a chance of confusing a naïve player. It even shows up online in small-stakes cash games: a player will hesitate for as long as possible ("9 seconds . . . 8 seconds . . . 7 seconds") before raising big with what inevitably proves to be the nuts or close to it.

Like a black hole warping space and time, big-bet poker has a distorting effect on tells in general—sometimes drawing them out or magnifying them, sometimes shrinking them to the size of a pinhead. Because the rewards for executing or picking off a bluff are so much greater, a reliable tell is worth much more than in limit. A strong player can pick apart a soft game using little more than position and tells. On the other hand, if you're up against tough opponents, nothing is what it seems; such players exhibit fewer tells than in limit, because they've put in more time hunting them down and eliminating them. And the few tells they *do* give off may well be fakes designed to trap foes who pride themselves on being observant.

Time itself becomes a weapon, but one that cuts both ways: a player can stall, hoping to pick up a tell from a weak opponent; but the very fact he's stalling may reveal that his own hand is weak. By comparison, limit play is much quicker and prolonged scrutiny is rare.

With these somewhat scary observations in mind, here are some common no-limit tells.

Before the Flop

Tell: Watching like a hawk, hoping to reraise.

Example: A $1/$2 no-limit cash game; the game has just gotten under way, and everyone's still playing pretty tight. The under-the-gun player limps, and the next two players fold. You notice that as the action goes around the table, the under-the-gun player is watching each player with extreme attention. It gets to you in the big blind with only three limpers all told. You find you're holding KQ—a terrible hand in no-limit, but maybe good enough to steal with: if you make a fair-sized raise, who among these tight limpers is going to have the guts to call you?

Explanation: Your problem here is the under-the-gun player. He may have been watching the way he did in hopes someone would raise, so he could reraise with the big pair he limped. Players who limp speculative hands up front are usually either resigned or relaxed, not predatory. Note that this tell *can* occur in limit, but it's much more dangerous when observed in no-limit.

What to do: Check your KQ and forget about stealing.

Tell: Sizing the raise to fit the hand.

Example: The same $1/$2 game. You're keeping track of who raises how much, and you begin to suspect that a particular player is raising about two times the big blind when he opens with hands like QJs, but from three to four times the big blind if he's raising with a pair of Tens or better.

Explanation: In small-stakes no-limit games, it's not uncommon for weak, action-oriented players to size their opening raises like this. Once you decipher the pattern, it's a huge tell.

What to do: You should get some good opportunities to steal preflop by reraising big whenever this guy's opening raise indicates weakness. Just be aware that the other players will eventually realize what's going on, at which point stealing will become a more complicated affair.

Tell: Hmm, should I raise?

Example: A player who normally is very quick to throw away her trash hands peeks at her hole cards when the action gets to her, and sits up. Her hand steals toward her chips, but then she stops herself and glances around the table. She casually tosses in the right amount of chips to limp with.

Explanation: Her first instinct was to raise, but she thought better of it. So what are her hole cards? If she's first to enter the pot, it's possible she's got a big pocket pair. In most cases, though, she'll have a marginal raising hand like AJs or a medium pocket pair. She's decided to see if she can flop a big hand cheaply rather than play a riskier line, but a limp-reraise is also a possibility if she's prone to gamble.

What to do: If you've got a drawing hand, go ahead and limp behind her. If you've got a hand you'd normally raise after a limper or two, you've got to take some extra thought as to what her action might be when it gets back around to her.

On the Flop

Tell: Heavy gunner, small bet, big trouble.

Example: You're up against a crafty, tough player; he hasn't shown down many hands so far this sit, largely because of his habit of making extremely large bets or raises on the flop after raising preflop. Nobody so far has stood the heat. Both you and he have good-sized stacks, so when he raises in early position, you feel justified calling with 7♠6♠ as dealer. The big blind calls too, and the three of you see a flop that comes K♥Q♠4♠. The preflop raiser ponders, then bets surprisingly small—only a quarter of the pot. Now it's your turn to ponder.

Explanation: Normally a small bet from the preflop raiser might represent a probe; in such a case you'd be justified in playing back hard, even though your flush draw is a small one. But this situation smells of danger. If this dynamite artist were up against more players, a probe might be plausible—but not when there's only two of you versus him. There's too good a chance here that he's flopped something massive, like top pair and the nut flush draw.

What to do: Consider folding and waiting for a better gambling opportunity.

Tell: Bully turns passive.

Example: A variation on the same theme. This time it's a loose-aggressive regular who's running over the game, a beer constantly in one hand and stacks of chips constantly in the other as he bulldozes the flop with big bets and raises. No one is catching hands against him, and he's filled up three racks by now, having bought in for just one. That's when you find you've caught black Aces under the gun.

You make your raise bigger than usual, hoping that everyone but Mr. Gonzo will fold. That's exactly what happens; on the button, he barely glances at his cards before tossing in his chips to call. Both blinds evacuate as your foe gets another beer from the waitress. The flop comes 993 and you check, planning to check-raise his inevitable bet. To your surprise, he docilely checks behind.

Explanation: Try to detach yourself from your warm feeling for your Aces. Instead, stop and ask yourself why this player has broken his usual pattern of trying to buy every pot. The most likely reason is because he's trapping with some hand that may be complete junk—except that it includes a Nine, giving him the trips. The second most likely reason is that he's got absolutely nothing here, but is planning to bluff at you on the turn if a face card or an Ace doesn't come.

What to do: When a player acts differently than you'd expect, sometimes it's just coincidence; other times, a sign of weakness. But very often, it's a sign of strength. You've got to weigh the chances he's trapping versus bluffing, and act accordingly. But given that he's got position on you and may well set you in for all your chips either way, a check and fold may end up being your best move.

Tell: Counting the pot with a draw.

Example: A $5/$5 game. A loose-aggressive player with about a grand in chips in front of him open-raises for four times the blind and gets called by the cutoff, a fairly passive player who has only about $650 in chips. You're in the big blind holding pocket Nines. As you've got more than one grand in chips yourself you could reraise to try to isolate the loose-aggressive player, but you don't like your position. Instead, you decide to call and await developments. The pot is now $65.

The flop comes T♥8♠5♣ and you check; the preflop raiser overbets the pot with a $100 bet. This seems curious, since twice so far you've seen him bet only between half to two-thirds of the pot when holding a legitimate hand. Further information comes from the cutoff—he stares at the pot, then at the big blind's stack, then fingers his own stack. Then he looks up and stares at the ceiling for a few seconds. Finally he calls the $100 bet.

Explanation: The cutoff was counting—and the only thing he could be counting here is whether the pot and his remaining stack give him the implied odds to call with a draw. He must think the preflop raiser has a made hand here, otherwise it would have made more sense for him to raise than just call.

What to do: Say that you don't agree with the cutoff—you read the first player as bluffing here with his unusually large bet. If you're right, then a big check-raise should win you the pot, knocking out the bluffer while depriving the cutoff of his implied odds. A raise to $300 seems about right.

Big Hands in Small Pots

Tell: Trying to keep the monster under wraps.

Example: An unraised, multiway pot—the kind of limpfest you often get in soft cash games. The ragged flop gets checked around. On the turn, a low straight flush becomes possible, but only if you hold exactly the right two-gapper hand of that suit. The two blinds check, and now it's up to the loose, naïve player who limped under the gun. As this player fingers his chips his hand trembles slightly. He pauses—a long pause that stretches out into a stall. Now he makes a big production of checking his hole cards. Another long pause. Then, reluctantly, he bets an amount almost exactly equal to the pot.

Explanation: You'll see this sort of thing fairly often in small-stakes cash games, where a fair number of pots get limped and big hands are generated with little means to collect a big pot. Here we've actually got many tells wrapped into one. First, the trembling hand. Second, the stall as he tries to figure out if there's any way to make money here. Third, the inspection of his hole cards, a threadbare attempt to convey weakness. And fourth, the pot-sized bet, a compromise between greed (he wants to make as much as he can) and fear (he's afraid everyone is going to fold if he bets anything at all). But frankly, any size bet would be suspect here after the first three tells.

Another common tell with a big hand in a small pot is the verbal tell. Say that the flop came K76 and a player calls a small bet. Now the turn brings another Seven; it's bet again, and this time the player raises, saying something like, "I don't think you have the King." It's an easy guess that what *he* holds is trips. You'll see these sorts of speech tells in limit, too, of course.

What to do: In our example with the straight flush, why would you ever call this guy?

Tell: Showing just one card.

Example: It's the river and the pot is about $40 in a $2/$4 game. The board is 47JJ5 and you hold A7 suited that you limped in with. You bet $12 on the flop, hoping to take it right there, but when you were called in two places you shut down. The turn was checked around; now the river is checked to the third player, who announces he'll show you one of his cards, a Four. "I think it's good," he says, as he bets $30. Your other opponent folds, leaving you to decide whether or not to contest the pot.

Explanation: He's got more than what he's showing you. When a player offers to reveal a card while a hand is still in progress, his goal is virtually always to mislead. In this case, it looks like he's begging for a call.

What to do: Muck your worthless Seven. Notice that here the fact that your opponent was last to act supports your read—with just a Four in a small pot with little incentive for action, would he really try to run a bluff? It's much more likely he'd take the free showdown and hope his hand was good. This is a fairly transparent gimmick, but you see it fairly often in unraised pots in no-limit— more than in limit, in my experience.

In the real-life hand this example was drawn from, the player with the A7 made the mistake of calling. All that bought him was the privilege of seeing his opponent's pocket Fours, for the small full house.

All-In—Does He Have It or Not?

Tell: Freezing but peeking.

Example: A big pot develops between you and the loose-aggressive player three seats to your right. You turn top two pair, but the river comes scary, making a straight *and* a flush possible. Now he goes all-in, which would put you nearly all-in, too. It would be a huge call for you to make, but a big laydown as well. He's not helping your decision: not only is he wearing shades, hiding his eyes from you, but he's gone into the freeze posture: totally motionless, staring straight ahead into space. You're not feeling great about your hand at this point. You flip up just the corners of your hole cards, but that doesn't help: still just top two pair. You look at your opponent once more, and that's when you realize there's something odd about his posture. At first glance he *appears* to be looking straight ahead, but actually he's sitting slightly twisted in his seat, so that his body points in your direction.

Explanation: All-in players who like to go motionless sometimes have a small tell: when they don't have it, they'll betray their fear that you're going to call by attempting to keep track of you—either by looking at you out of the corner of their eye whenever they think you're not looking, or, as in this example, by involuntarily turning their body ever so slightly to point at you. I've seen a surprising number of top tournament players display this tell on one occasion or another, including Carlos Mortensen, winner of the Main Event at the 2001 World Series of Poker.

What to do: His posture mandates a call here.

Tell: Unfeigned drama.

Example: A sloppy $1/$2 game at the local club. A loose, inexperienced young player makes it $25 in late position after several limpers. He gets one caller, the equally inexperienced young man in the big blind. The flop comes AK7; the preflop raiser bets another $25, about half the pot. The big blind calls, hunched over in his seat as if lacking confidence. The turn brings another Ace and the preflop raiser bets the pot, about $100. Again the big blind calls, but more slowly this time; even as he calls he seems to be sitting taller in his seat. The river is a third Ace! The big blind seems like he's either about to explode or burst into tears as he pushes all-in for his remaining $140. The preflop raiser immediately calls. The big blind flips over AQ for—what else?—quads. The preflop raiser in a daze flips over Kings, giving him a losing Kings full of Aces.

Explanation: The preflop raiser here is caught in a classic poker dilemma: he's hit a huge hand by flopping a set of Kings, but his excitement blinds him from seeing the obvious tells displayed on the turn and the river by the big blind. Contributing to the problem is that quads are a relatively rare hand in terms of probabilities. But when the signs are right, you have to adjust the probabilities to a new reality, not use them as an excuse to give your money away.

What to do: It's hard, but there *are* ways to improve your decision-making skills when in the grip of strong emotion. We'll discuss a few of these in chapter 7, "Becoming a Poker Psychic."

CHAPTER 6

TEST YOUR TELL DETECTOR

Here's a brief photo quiz to test what you've learned so far. The answers are at the end of this chapter. Good luck!

Sequence 1

You're in late middle position in a hold'em game, and the player to your left is peeking at his hole cards.

Now he's done looking. It's folded around to you. You find you've got AT; should you limp in, or raise?

Sequence 2

A small-ante seven-stud game. The player across the table from you is checking his hole cards; he has an Ace doorcard.

Now he's waiting for the action to get to him. You look at your own cards and find you have split Jacks to go with your Nine kicker. How should you play them?

Sequence 3

This player usually cuts his chips neatly and pushes them forward when betting.

But this time he's splashed his chips as he bets. What's the story?

Sequence 4

The big blind sees the flop.

Here's his reaction a second later. Meanwhile you haven't flopped too badly yourself—top pair, medium kicker. What's your plan?

Sequence 5

This no-limit hold'em player appears flummoxed by his opponent's pot-sized bet. It's taking him a long time to decide what to do.

At last, he shrugs as if to say, "What the heck?" and pushes all-in. Should his opponent call?

Sequence 6

The flop has just hit, and these two players are checking it out.

One of them loves it, the other hates it. Can you tell which and why?

Sequence 7

The player on the left has gone all-in. Should the other player call?

Again the player on the left has gone all-in. How about this time—should the other player call?

Sequence 8

Before the flop, the player in the small blind is gabbing happily away.

By the time the turn comes, he's head-up with the big blind and has fallen silent. He checks. What should the big blind do?

Sequence 9

The river has paired the turn card. The first player has just made a hefty bet, and the Yankees fan is checking his hole cards.

Now the Yankees fan is raising. What should the first player do?

Sequence 10

A weak player has just seen his river card in stud. How does he like it?

Same player, different river card. This time, how does he like it?

Answers
Sequence 1

Question: You're in late middle position in a hold'em game. In the first photo the player to your left is peeking at his hole cards. In the second photo he's done looking. It's folded around to you. You've got AT; should you limp in, or raise?

Answer: This actor is pretending he doesn't like what he saw, which means he *does* like it. He's probably planning on raising himself. Given that your AT is likely weaker than whatever he likes so much, and that he'll have position on you throughout the hand, your best move here is a fold.

Sequence 2

Question: A small-ante seven-stud game. The player across the table from you has an Ace doorcard. He checks his hole cards, then sits waiting for the action to get to him. You've got split Jacks to go with your Nine kicker; how should you play them?

Answer: Dump your Jacks. This guy likes his split Aces so much he's already loading up to raise.

Sequence 3

Question: Usually this player cuts his chips neatly and pushes them forward when betting. But this time he's splashed them as he bets. What's the story?

Answer: The splash most likely signals either a bluff or semi-bluff, though it could also signal an unusually strong hand. You'll need to keep watching his betting

101

patterns and the cards he shows down to establish a definitive correlation. Once you do, it's money in the bank for you.

Sequence 4

Question: The big blind sees the flop and immediately looks at his chips. You haven't flopped too badly yourself—top pair, medium kicker. It's to you; what should you do here?

Answer: The chip-glance is the giveaway—he loves this flop. If he's a reasonable player and you don't have any draws or other reasons to hang around, plan on check-folding here.

Sequence 5

Question: This no-limit hold'em player appears flummoxed by his opponent's pot-sized bet. At last, he shrugs as if to say, "What the heck?" and pushes all-in. Should his opponent call?

Answer: Without an extremely strong hand, his opponent should fold. The stall and the acting job combined make it likely this guy has either the nuts or close to it.

Sequence 6

Question: The flop has just hit, and these two players are checking it out. One of them loves it, the other hates it. Who's who and why?

Answer: The guy loves it, hence he instinctively glances away to pretend he couldn't care less. The gal hates it, hence she instinctively keeps staring at the flop like it's speaking to her.

Sequence 7

Question: In the first photo, the player on the left is all-in. Should the second player call? Same situation in the second photo; how about now?

Answer: A call would be a mistake in the first photo; he's got the goods here. We know this partly because we get to see the second photo, which shows us how he acts when he *doesn't* have the goods: under the strain of bluffing, he can't stop himself from taking a nervous peek at his opponent.

Sequence 8

Question: Before the flop, the player in the small blind is gabbing happily away. By the time the turn comes, he's head-up with the big blind and has fallen silent. Now he checks. What should the big blind do?

Answer: A lot depends on the nature of the small blind's silence. If he seems genuinely dejected, he may have missed his draw on the turn or otherwise feel it's time to fold to a bet. If, on the other hand, he's acting, then his silence may be part of a trap. The big blind will have to use his judgement.

Sequence 9

Question: The river has paired the turn card. The first player bets; the Yankees fan double-checks his hole cards, then raises. What should the first player do?

Answer: The double-check is the tell here. Unless the first player holds trips or better himself, he should fold.

Sequence 10

Question: In the first photo, a weak player has just seen his river card in stud. How does he like it? The second photo shows the same player, but a different river card. How does he like it this time?

Answer: He loves it the first time, hence he sits up straight and beams. He hates it the second time, hence he slumps. The fact that he's a weak player makes this tell especially reliable here. A more sophisticated player might try to act these tells in reverse.

CHAPTER 7

BECOMING A POKER PSYCHIC

This may be the most useful chapter in this book—but only if you're willing to take the time to learn things not normally thought of as related to poker. We're going to talk here not about tells per se, but about how to increase your ability to detect tells. It's one thing to learn a list of tells—similar to the lists we've presented in the last few chapters—but it's another to be able to reliably spot these and other tells in the heat of the action.

The truth is that even the very best players, renowned for their ability to seemingly read their opponents' minds, often make terrible blunders in the face of obvious tells. And if players of this caliber can make such bad mistakes, how much more likely is it that you and I will do the same? I know from my own experience that there are days when I spot tells easily and other days when I might as well be blindfolded.

Once you gain a certain degree of competency in picking up tells, what you really need are techniques to free your innate poker intelligence by removing the obstacles to that intelligence. Fortunately, such techniques exist. In this chapter we're going to talk about:

- ♣ Learning to develop and trust your intuition.
- ♣ Becoming more systematic about how you accumulate player information to feed that intuition. I call this building your poker database.
- ♣ Cultivating clear vision, so your emotions and thought processes don't obstruct what you should be seeing. Very tough, very worthwhile.

♣ Learning more about the far frontier of tells: micro expressions and posture leakage. We mentioned these briefly in chapter 2, but now we'll take a closer look.

The Nature of Intuition

We use intuition every day of our lives, whether we're conscious of it or not. When we label it as such, it sounds mysterious, but of course it's not mysterious at all, rather a basic function of the human mind.

Aside from good poker players, who else needs to rely on intuition? Well, how about the jury consultants who help lawyers choose potentially sympathetic jurors, while excluding jurors who may be hostile? This has become a fairly hot niche, and more than one such consultant has written a book on how to read people. One of these consultants is Jo-Ellan Dimitrius, who helped select the jury that acquitted O. J. Simpson. Her book, cowritten with Mark Mazzarella, is called *Reading People*. In it, she gives as concise and useful a definition of intuition as you'll find anywhere:

> What we call intuition is nearly always the surfacing of a submerged memory, a barely noticed event, or some combination of the two. That "feeling" doesn't come to us over the cosmic ether, but drifts up from our own subconscious. This means that all we have to do to greatly improve our intuitive abilities is to find new ways to gather information, store it, and retrieve it from our subconscious.

Reread the last sentence in the quote. It describes a perfect strategy for intuitive jury selection, and a perfect strategy for picking up tells in poker.

Dimitrius' Three Steps for Developing the Intuitive Process

Let's start first with improving how we retrieve information from our subconscious once we've stored it. It's logical to start here because, in fact, all of us already have a great deal of this information squirreled away; the problem is we don't always trust it. To put it another way, tapping your intuition is largely a matter of developing trust. You'll improve your ability to recognize individual and involuntary tells through the small bits of information that float to the surface of consciousness—the barely noticed event of the player handling his chips differently this time than last, for example.

Dimitrius suggests a three-step process for listening to intuition and deciphering its message. I've modified this process to fit the poker table, as follows:

1. **Recognize and respect your intuition in the first place.** It's true that you need to be thinking about a great many things at the table. But if you want to pick up on tells, you've got to split off at least part of your consciousness so that when you feel the breath of intuition at your ear, you listen. Don't get so wrapped up in your calculations that you ignore that little voice when it whispers, "Hmm, something doesn't seem genuine here," or "Why is he calling? Why isn't he folding?"

It's all too easy to silence intuition by ignoring it—even in cases where it's not whispering, but yelling. For example, say a complete rock starts raising and reraising on the early streets in a high-low stud game. We're showing a King doorcard (in fact, we've got split Kings), while he's only got a Ten doorcard, no good for a low. So what's going on here? Our intuition rings the alarm, and it takes only a moment of conscious thought to realize we're likely in deep trouble; the only hands he'd jam with in this spot are pocket Aces or trip Tens. If we want to play our hand badly enough, however, we'll find a way to suppress this knowledge. The moment we shut off our thinking brain, intuition becomes unavailable, too. It's only at the end of the hand, when the rock shows his Aces up or Tens full of whatever, that full access returns to both the conscious and the subconscious mind. At that point we wonder how we could have been so stupid.

2. **Identify exactly what it is your intuition is telling you.** It's not enough to have a funny feeling—you have to stop and ask yourself what the feeling means. In the example of the rock jamming with a Ten doorcard, the meaning is pretty obvious, but in a lot of cases it's more subtle. For example, it might just be a feeling of danger, or else the reverse—a sudden suspicion that a perceived danger isn't actually as threatening as it seems.

3. **Review the evidence.** If you can't immediately tie your intuition to something concrete, you'll have to do some investigating. Replay the hand, looking for

patterns and inconsistencies; ask yourself if you're recognizing a pattern from similar hands in the past, whether with this opponent or in general. Also consider your opponent's facial expression and posture to see if he's radiating any obvious tells you might have been ignoring. Ideally, the nagging voice will suddenly turn into a conscious realization. If so, you can now factor it into your decision, along with pot odds and other information.

As always, you're looking for information that has the potential to change the decision you would have made otherwise. In the case of the high-low stud player with the Ten doorcard, you normally wouldn't be folding split Kings just starting out, so listening to the alarm signal could save you a lot of money. If you had a strong low, the information wouldn't be as immediately valuable—although it still might affect how you play the hand on later streets.

Other Tips for Developing Intuition

Here are a few simple things you can do to honor your intuition and stretch it further than usual.

- ♣ If you get an immediate read, trust your gut; don't start second-guessing yourself. For this to work, you can't be afraid to guess wrong sometimes. Every wrong guess will help build correct instincts for the future.
- ♣ Experiment now and then with wearing headphones, even if you normally don't. Don't space out to your

favorite music; listen to something bland, or even to white noise. Then tune into the mime show around you to see if you learn anything new. By shutting off your ears, you're hoping to develop your ability to read faces, postures, and other visual tells.

♣ If you haven't already, get a hold of some of the DVDs put out by the World Poker Tour and the World Series of Poker. Don't watch them for entertainment, but for the tells displayed by great players and mediocre players alike. To really give yourself a workout, cut a piece of paper to size and tape it over the part of the screen where players' hole cards are revealed (yes, it sounds geeky, but it only takes a minute to do). Then turn down the sound so you don't hear the announcers. Go through a hand and see what you spot, then replay it with the paper off and the sound up to see if you were right.

Building Your Poker Database

As Jo-Ellan Dimitrius points out in her definition of intuition, the better your database of information about people, the better your intuitive reads will be. What this means is that you need to be observing all the time—and in as systematic a way as possible. You've got to know what to look for and develop the habit of looking for it. And when you find it, you've got to take extra care to file the information away in usable form for the future. Sometimes all you've got to work with is your memory, but you can also make use of such devices as a player notebook or poker journal.

Being observant in poker requires watching players as much as you can. That doesn't mean constantly staring them down in search of tells. Your time at the table will include a lot of other activities as well, including calculating odds and outs; watching the action so as to make educated guesses about who's got what, as well as to pick up on betting patterns; monitoring the overall flow of the game as players change; watching yourself to keep tabs on your physical and mental state; and reviewing decisions you made in the previous hand. And then of course there's all the extra stuff of interacting with the other players and otherwise relaxing. Even if you're a pro you need to do some relaxing, whether at or away from the table—just sitting there trying to concentrate on poker and nothing else will fry your brain in short order.

Even with all this going on, you still want to watch players quite a bit, both for betting patterns and for tells. Obviously, the best time to watch is when you're not in a hand because then you can devote all your concentration to the task, undistracted by decision making or emotion. Aside from tells and betting patterns per se, you should also stay alert for clues to opponents' personalities, their motivation for playing and their beliefs about poker, whether they're winning or losing, how much they feel they can afford to lose, the mood they're in, how they feel about you and your play, and so on. All of this is valuable information.

Of course you can witness all of this without bothering to studiously think about it. That's what we do every day of our lives: we watch what's going on around us without really paying attention unless we're forced to. But if you don't think about what you're observing, you usually won't remember it. In the Sherlock Holmes story *A Scandal in Bohemia*, Holmes tells Watson that he knows there are 17 steps leading up to their flat on Baker Street because he has both seen and observed, whereas Watson has only seen. It's the same in poker. You stand a better chance of developing both conscious and subconscious memories if you think about what you're seeing instead of merely letting it happen.

Tips for Aiding Observation

The following ideas are part of standard procedure for many advanced players. If you haven't tried them yet yourself, they can be very helpful.

♣ As mentioned, you can keep a player notebook. This is especially important if you're playing for significant stakes and you frequent a regular cardroom. When you make your first note on a particular player, include his name or his nickname, as well as where he's from; this will help you remember him in the future. If necessary, briefly describe his appearance, for the same reason. (Sure, you could snap a picture of him with your camera phone, but that's a good way to get yourself banned from the cardroom.) After that, you're ready to enter any and all data you learn about him, together with a note as to the game type, limit, date, and so on. Generally I do this away from the table so I can concentrate, but lots of people scribble things at the table, so that's okay, too; just have a good excuse handy if someone asks what you're doing.

♣ A poker journal is a good place to record any generic tells you've witnessed, along with your analysis of hands you played well or badly, ideas for improving your play in the future, and so on. Keeping such a journal is a matter of preference, of course; if you're blessed with a photographic memory for poker, as many top pros claim to be, a journal is unnecessary. Personally, I haven't yet met a poker player who truly has that kind of memory, but I do know of at least one chess player who has it—proof enough for me that the talent exists.

♣ Spend more time listening to conversations and comments than responding. And when you listen, listen between the lines. Be alert to what other players say about you and really consider the implications, rather than getting defensive and justifying yourself to yourself. Often other players know more about you than you think; just as often they're reacting to their own assumptions or to your short-term results, not to reality. Try to sort out the differences. Also listen for the motivations behind any comments directed at you: Are they angle-shooting? Fishing for information, and if so, what? Are they just having a bad day?

♣ This last tip is only if you're relatively new to live poker: simply put, don't be afraid to watch the other players. At first it may seem rude to openly study someone, but since everyone does it, it's generally accepted. It's true that some players really don't like to be watched, but usually these players are long-term losers who don't know much about poker. Be tactful with them anyway. In the long run it won't be a problem, as the more you watch players, the better you'll get at appearing not to do so. Related to this, I highly recommend avoiding staring contests; they're distracting and don't yield much in the way of useful information, so don't be afraid to look away if someone locks eyes with you. Lastly, as you watch, keep in mind that those players who are actors will wait to put on their show until they feel they're being watched. Look also for their unguarded moments, which tend to be when the action isn't on them.

Specific Things to Look For

Sherlock Holmes counted the steps up to his flat, but that was just to show off. As a poker player, what should you be keeping your eye on? We've discussed most of these items already in the chapter on generic tells, but it doesn't hurt to repeat them here.

- ♣ Watch faces, not the cards. You can always look at the cards later. For example, don't watch the flop being dealt in hold'em, but instead watch faces to see who looks away or at their chips, who peeks at their hole cards, and so on.

- ♣ Spend some time watching just hands, not faces. You're looking for betting tempo and chip tells. With tempo, it's often the case that a fast bet means weakness and a slow bet spells strength. But sometimes it can be the reverse, so watch for individual variations.

♣ Make it a habit to always look left to catch telegraphs. Make your glance casual and brief; if possible, use your peripheral vision.

♣ Watch players just before they fold. A surprising number will drop their poker faces at this time and display shrugs, rueful smiles, and other involuntary signals indicating the release of tension; they may also handle their cards differently as they get ready to muck them. Then notice if these players display the same cues when they check with the intent to fold, versus checking with the intent to call or check-raise.

Should You Talk to Elicit a Tell?

Before we leave this section, let's talk about one commonly used strategy for gaining information—asking questions of your opponent. This goes beyond simply stalling to active probing. Usually this is done to determine if an opponent might be bluffing; and as we've noted, it's more common to no-limit, where players are allowed to take more time because the consequences of any single decision are greater than in limit.

A few of the top tournament players probe—Phil Hellmuth Jr. and Daniel Negreanu, for example—but many more don't. When was the last time you saw Chris Ferguson, Barry Greenstein, or Gus Hansen start yapping at their opponent? To some degree, this is a matter of personality: Negreanu's whole game is built around him being a pest, as he'll cheerfully confess, so talking to opponents is a natural fit for him. Chris Ferguson, on the other hand, not only bases his play on game theory, but seems to be a shy and courteous fellow in general, so talking would be out of character both strategically and personally.

When your opponent is all-in, talking can't immediately hurt you. But if he's not yet all-in, your attempt to probe may say more about your hand than his. If he doesn't bother to reply and you can't elicit any obvious tells, then you're on the losing side of the information exchange.

Talking can backfire on you even after the hand is over, especially if opponents know they can easily put you on tilt. A great example of this was a head-up hand I saw on television between Annie Duke and Phil Hellmuth Jr. The event was one of these single-table affairs, with only big-name players invited. Hellmuth had flopped top pair on a ragged board, but Duke had flopped two pair. She made a big raise on the turn, and at this point Hellmuth started yapping, telling her how strong he was and what a big laydown he'd be making. Duke didn't say anything.

Hellmuth then made the laydown, which was correct on his part, but that's when his probe backfired. Before mucking, Duke decided to show him just one of her two cards—the one that had made her middle pair. She didn't bother showing her other card for top pair. Hellmuth kept blabbing out loud as he slowly went on tilt. Had she made a move at him with just middle pair? Had he mucked what was really the best hand? On and on and on.

A few hands later he self-destructed entirely and busted out, leaving Duke with all the chips. Of course, Hellmuth is known for being combustible, but Duke probably wouldn't have even thought to play with his mind like this if he hadn't opened the door by talking.

Hellmuth isn't alone. I see many recreational no-limit players who attempt to probe with a question, start rambling, and finish by convincing themselves of whatever it is they most want to believe. Information gained: zero. Players like that should keep their mouths shut and concentrate on improving the technical aspects of their game. They're just not ready to be the next Daniel Negreanu.

Cultivating Clear Vision

Why do even great players make so many mistakes late in the play of a hand, frequently missing obvious tells in the process? Generally it's because they're thinking too hard about their own hand, or about a decision they're about to make that will require a great deal of risk, such as a big bluff with no hand. They're so caught up in their thought process that they can't step outside of it.

With most of us, emotion also plays an obscuring role. Say, for example, we've flopped a big hand like top two pair; very often we stop looking for tells and start gloating over the pot we're confident we're going to win. If something weird happens, like a runner-runner that gives our opponent the nut hand, we won't see it. We may think we're alert and accounting for every variable, but this is seldom the case. These situations call for an enormous degree of cool, and few people have it.

One person who obviously does is Doyle Brunson. On at least one occasion in his lengthy career, Brunson laid down Aces full versus not one but two opponents with quads. Few if any recreational players would have the presence of mind to see they were beat and make the same laydown, and not too many pros either. Brunson made his decision on a logical review of the betting, not on tells, but the principle is the same: you've got to get out of your own way before you can see clearly what to do.

Following are some strategies for cultivating clear vision:

♣ Minimize non-poker factors that create emotional stress. This includes everything from staying in shape and eating right to avoiding stakes that are too high and will make you anxious.

♣ Learn how to consciously relax at the table in stressful situations. Breathing exercises can be a big help, as can visualization exercises. See appendix B for books and other tools that teach such techniques.

♣ Take frequent breaks. When you come back from a break, don't sit right back down, but spend a minute or two watching the table from 10 feet away or so. This conscious decision to allow a distance between you and the action will help you create an emotional distance as well. When you sit back down, stay aware of that emotional distance for a while. Learn to recognize this feeling so you can call it back on command.

♣ When deep in a hand, pretend for a moment that you don't know your hole cards and are playing in the dark. Then review the action as dispassionately as possible to see what signals have been sent back and forth, whether through the action or through tells. I suggest you first practice this exercise on routine hands before venturing it with a big hand.

♣ Pretend you're playing this hand for a friend and have nothing personally at stake, either to gain or to lose. Make the best decisions you can for your friend. Think of what you'll tell him after the hand is over.

♣ If you're serious about gaining control of your emotions and your concentration over the long-term, take up a form of meditation or yoga. You'll discover both how to tune into feelings or thoughts you usually ignore and how to forget your self (quite literally) so as to see others more clearly, without your usual assumptions. This will help you in daily life as well as at the poker table.

Micro Expressions, Leakages, and Other Advanced Tells

We touched on micro expressions and posture leakages briefly in chapter 2; now let's look at them in more detail. They're a potentially rich source of tells, but it takes special skills to read them that most of us don't have and aren't normally likely to develop.

Micro expressions are the brainchild of psychologist and researcher Paul Ekman. Ekman reports that even people who are acting or trying to keep a poker face will often flash a micro expression in the split second between learning new information and covering up. If you're fearful, your upper eyelids will rise up for a moment while your mouth stretches into a grimace; if you're angry, your eyebrows will lower for a split second as your eyes flare and your mouth tightens. It happens so fast you can't control it and probably aren't even aware of it. Ekman speculates that we leak these momentary expressions because during human evolution, it was more useful than not for others in our family or tribal group to know what we were feeling. Put simply, group survival often depended on it.

Even though micros are basic to our nature as human beings, few of us are able to reliably see and interpret them on a conscious level. Among this skilled minority, Ekman reports, are Buddhist monks, elite law enforcement officers, and psychologists such as himself who study deception. Elite poker players probably possess a similar ability. The good news is that although most people skilled at reading micros aren't sure how they do it, Ekman has established that it's something that can be consciously taught and learned.

Suggestions for learning to read micro expressions:

♣ Purchase and study the training CD-ROM marketed by Ekman. It's not an actual video, but rather a series of animated photographs of faces, with the micro expressions "glued on" by photographic manipulation. They flash by very quickly, just as micros do in real life. Real video would have been better, but it's still an effective teaching tool. See appendix B for information on ordering this material.

♣ Go a step further and record a television program where people are displaying strong emotions. Then play it back at slow speed and watch for the momentary distortion of faces before larger emotions emerge; these small distortions are micro expressions. Or consider trying it with your favorite poker tournament DVD. If it seems like a lot of effort, just keep your investigations brief—a half hour is probably plenty to start with.

♣ Read Ekman's book, *Emotions Revealed* (again, see appendix B for more information). Be warned: it's not a poker book and may not seem immediately applicable. On the plus side, you'll learn a lot not only about micro expressions, but about how our emotional state influences our thinking. At the poker table, you can use this knowledge for both greater self-control and greater empathy. These qualities may seem contradictory, but in the long run they'll help your game.

Facial and Posture Leakages You May See at the Table

The following leakages are similar to micros because they're so hard to fake and because they let emotions slip that the player is doing his best to conceal. With some exceptions, they typically occur when a player is under greater pressure than usual. (You may remember that the hand between Scott Wilson and Phil Gordon in chapter 2 featured the first three of these four leakages.)

♣ *Either partially averting the body from an opponent, or partially pointing the body toward an opponent.* The first may indicate uncertainty, shame, or fear; the second may indicate concern. Remember, these are partial turnings of the body; a full turn-away, involving the whole body, is more likely a deliberate action. For example, a player with a strong hand may turn his body or his head fully away from an opponent in order to avoid discouraging a bet.

♣ *Unintentional lowering of the head as the player struggles to make a tough decision.* Again, you've got to distinguish this from deliberate turtle-heading as part of a strategy to seem weak or minimize information. The unintentionally lowered head occurs because our neck muscles tend to slacken momentarily when we're feeling shame or confusion.

♣ *Embarrassed smile, reflecting shame.* Again, this is a slow leakage that the player will try to prevent. It won't be a big, full smile with eye contact; it won't be a grin.

♣ *Wrinkled nose, as a signal of contempt or dominance.* May go along with a frown of concentration. You'll often see this when the player has a strong hand and subconsciously wants his opponents to know it's strong—for example, a player raising preflop with AK may show this expression, whereas he won't with AA or KK. So may a player who's betting top pair on the flop, whereas he won't show it with a much stronger hand like a set. Strong players exhibit this tell infrequently, if at all; they're more interested in keeping you guessing for the entire sit than in making sure their AK or top pair holds up in any given hand.

CHAPTER 8

AVOIDING TELLS YOURSELF

Do I have any tells when playing poker? You bet. According to my closest friend in the poker world, I tend to talk more when I have a good hand, put my chips in the pot differently when I have a weak hand, and get a certain indefinable glow on my face whenever I hit a monster (probably this "glow" is me sitting up in my seat more, while flashing a micro expression). On the other hand, I've more than once surprised this same friend into guessing wrong about my hand—sometimes with successful fake tells, sometimes by managing to suppress my monster glow in a situation where he was sure I was crushed but in fact was slowplaying the nuts.

Being pretty emotional in general at the poker table, I've had to work harder than most on both suppression and deception. Fortunately, I've made a lot of progress in recent years, relying in part on the tips you'll find in this chapter. Given that some of the best players in the world leak tells now and then, this is an area that we can probably all work on. However, just as it's possible to get too wrapped up in looking for tells, it's also possible to get too obsessive about trying to suppress them, so we'll address this issue as well.

To Act or Not to Act? That Is the Question

You'll recall that in chapter 2 we talked about the stages all good poker players go through (but not all bad players) in dealing with tells. In Stages 1 and 2, we're pretty much clueless. In Stage 3, we get the inspired idea that we can best deceive by acting weak when strong, strong when weak. This often gets us interested in trying to read other players as weak or strong, too; we've reinvented for ourselves the old adage that poker is less a game of calculation than a "people game."

By the time we reach Stage 4, we've worn ourselves out with acting. It's hard work, and rarely seems to fool our more experienced opponents. So we decide to go the opposite way, and behave exactly the same way with every hand; that way, we'll keep our opponents off balance by forcing them to guess. At this point we may downplay the importance of tells in general, preferring to put most of our attention on betting patterns, correctly calculating the odds, and so on.

Only the best players reach Stage 5. These players have learned to attach just the right importance to tells, neither too much nor too little. They've also learned how to fake tells in a more convincing manner than the bad acting jobs found in Stage 3. However, they'll only engage in such fakery against opponents who they suspect are actively looking for tells in the first place. Compared to the rest of us, Stage 5 players waste very little energy.

This is good background to have, but let's look at things a little differently now—not from the point of view of how poker players evolve, but in terms of selecting a personal strategy or style for deception. Put this way, you've actually got four styles to choose from.

Style 1: Break a Leg

You can choose to be an actor as much of the time as possible. But as we've said, this not only takes a lot of work, but is very difficult to pull off. Basically, you end up generating as many tells by acting as you would by playing in the most naïve manner possible. So we'll rule this option out. Note that we're talking about acting at the simplest level, not the more advanced tactic of creating convincing reverse tells.

Style 2: Get Crazy

You won't find this style in the five-stage model I've given for the evolution of poker players, for the simple reason that very few players ever try it. The player most associated with this approach in poker legend is "Crazy Mike" Caro, the author of *The Book of Tells*. As one of the best five-card draw players ever, Caro maintained a near-continuous impersonation of a lunatic—jabbering nonsense, making supposedly crazy plays, listening to a tape recorder to tell him when to bet or raise, and so on.

By generating so much static, Caro effectively concealed any genuine tells he might happen to emit. However, this was only a side effect. The real goal of his clowning was to dupe weaker players into seeing him as crazy—a loose, wild fool who constantly bluffed and should be called as often as possible—when, in fact, he actually bluffed very little. Here we can see that his approach solved one of the biggest problems in draw poker: how to get as much action as possible on your big hands with only two rounds of betting.

In hold'em and seven-card stud, however, big hands usually get much more action, so this strategy is worth a lot less. Even so, there are still a handful of players who act as zany as they can as often as they can. A prime example is tournament player Phil "the Unabomber" Laak. At various times during and between hands, Laak will shroud his entire head in his sweatshirt hood until only his nose shows, sprint around the table, do the wave, flop onto the floor and do sit-ups, jabber excitedly, hug other players, and so on.

Laak is probably having a fun time, but is he eliminating tells? No. In fact, if you watch, he displays a great many tells for anyone who cares to pick up on them. For example, if he flops a great hand, he may lower his head onto the table and keep it there. Although this may confuse a gullible opponent, it's actually the classic tell of acting weak when strong. Meanwhile, all that energy he puts into acting crazy is energy not available for thinking. Laak is a talented and engaging fellow, but this may be one reason he's not in the top echelon of tournament players.

Another variation of this strategy involves not so much physical motion as a constant stream of talk. A player with this style is usually trying to distract other players and make himself more difficult to read. Again, though, most talkers generate more tells than they conceal. For example, when they actually have to concentrate on a tough decision, they usually fall silent to do so. Amarillo Slim was a famous talker, and he did pretty well in his day; but even then he was never regarded as being in the same weight class as Johnny Moss, Doyle Brunson, Puggy Pearson, or other top players.

The sheer energy required to keep up the crazy or distracting style is probably one reason that most players never attempt it; another is the embarrassment most of us would feel at making a fool of ourselves in public. The final blow is that it offers minimal rewards for action games like hold'em and stud. Players with this approach are sometimes able to dominate soft games, but they'll usually end up losing in tough games.

Style 3: Become a Robot

This is the style of choice for most of us. Again, it's nothing more than attempting to suppress tells by making your facial expressions, chip-handling, and body language as consistent as possible from hand to hand. Compared to the acting and crazy styles, it requires much less energy while offering better potential results. As we've seen, a player like Chris Ferguson takes this style to an extreme, but with considerable benefits: the less he gives away, the less energy he has to expend. The style also has a calming effect, since the less emotion you display, the less emotion you actually feel. This can only benefit your poker. And all that energy and time you save is energy and time you can devote to thinking. David Sklansky wouldn't be the brilliant thinker he is at the table if he had to spend a lot of time acting or dancing around.

Another advantage to this style is that it's appropriate at every limit and in every type of game. You can play low-limit poker and do well with it; you can also sit in the highest-stakes games around and do equally well with it, as players like Barry Greenstein and Chip Reese have demonstrated over the years.

131

The key to this style is working methodically and ruthlessly to eliminate your remaining tells. I'll shortly be giving you some tips for doing just that.

Style 4: Become a Robot That Can Go in Reverse

Essentially we're talking Stage 5 here: getting creative enough to generate a reverse or fake tell at the right time against the right player. If this appeals to you, it doesn't automatically make you a Stage 5 player, though. For that, you genuinely have to evolve from poker amoeba to poker savant, not just latch on to a gimmick because it's expedient. There are a lot of recreational players with nothing better to do than attempt fake tells now and then. And of course, it works now and then too, even though they're not at Stage 5.

As we've noted, part of the trick is to know when the effort of faking or reversing a tell is worth it. Stage 5 players have a good instinct for who's watching and who's not. If you haven't yet developed that instinct, I'd advise waiting until you do. On the other hand, if in the middle of a hand you get an inspiration for what seems like a beautiful and fitting reverse tell, by all means try it and see what happens.

An example of a typical reverse tell is one suggested by T. J. Cloutier: when he's made a huge bet or raise with a big hand and his opponent is staring him down, trying to determine if he's bluffing, Cloutier will sometimes swallow hard and look away. Another reverse bluff in the same situation would be to cover your mouth with your hand.

The best reverse tells are individual in nature: if you've been caught bluffing and you can remember your body language, facial expression, words, or anything else that might have stuck in your opponent's mind, you can try to repeat this same behavior when you make a similar big bet—only the next time you'll have the goods. Phil Hellmuth Jr. has said that he does this often and that it works.

Become Self-Aware

I'm assuming at this point that you've chosen to become a stone-faced, ice-cold, radiator-fluid-for-blood robot like the rest of us. Since it offers the best cost-to-benefit ratio of the four styles we've looked at, it's only natural to become unnatural.

So now we're a robot. Yet we still experience nagging grimaces, involuntary changes in posture or vocal register at the wrong moment, and other betraying signs of humanity. How do we get rid of these? The basic principle is to become more self-aware. You can't change a behavior you don't know about; it's only after you spot it that you can take action.

Slow It Down

The first principle of self-discovery is an easy one: don't be in such a rush at the table. Even in limit poker, you can slow down your decisions by taking 10 seconds when normally you'd rap out a bet or a call. Don't do this to excess—there's no point in irritating other players—but do it enough that you begin to create more mental space for yourself. Use this mental space not only to improve your thought process, but to observe your body language, posture, gestures, and what your face feels like. Also get in touch with any emotions that may be lurking; when we're in a hurry, we're usually only half-aware of how a feeling like frustration or anticipation is distorting our thoughts and decisions.

An additional advantage of slowing down is that this in and of itself will minimize many tells. Eagerness often betrays a big hand; if you always act at the same, deliberate pace, opponents will have a harder time reading you as weak or strong.

Monitor Your Voice and How Much You Talk

Listen to yourself when you talk; that's rule number one. Rule number two is to talk less. Doyle Brunson has written that during a big hand, he'd refuse to let anyone engage him in conversation; it's not a bad idea for you to do the same.

This is a rule I need to follow myself in my own play. As I've noted, like many players, I tend to talk too much with a big hand. Words come more easily when you're confident; combine this with the natural instinct to wheedle an opponent into calling by hook or by crook, and you've got an easy-to-spot tell. Keeping your mouth shut will help you avoid this and similar giveaways.

Handle Your Hole Cards Right

You should already know this, but if you don't, make sure you treat your hole cards the same way whether they're garbage or gold. Don't put a chip on a pocket pair you intend to play, but leave uncovered a trash hand you intend to muck; don't habitually pull good cards toward you and leave bad cards hanging out there where they could accidentally get flipped over or mucked by the dealer. The way to discover whether you do this or not is simply to monitor yourself. Probably you should do this during a sit at a fairly low limit or in some other unpressured setting.

The other question about hole cards is, of course, when to look at them. The standard advice is to look only when the action gets to you, thereby eliminating the possibility you'll telegraph your intentions. This advice is good as far as it goes, but it has a drawback: you'll be forced to make your decision about your hand when all eyes are upon you, and when time is relatively short.

If, on the other hand, you look at your hole cards as soon as you get them, you'll have that much more time to process them mentally and come to a decision *before* the action gets to you.

It's also notable that even as good a player as T. J. Cloutier likes to look at his hole cards immediately—not so he can get extra time for mulling them over, but so he can thereafter scrutinize the other players for tells without having to think about his own cards. If it works for him, it can work for you.

Which way do I go on this issue? If I'm playing well, I tend not to look at my hole cards until the action gets to me; among other things I find this makes it easier to count the bets going into the pot. But if I've been playing too loosely before the flop, I find that looking at my cards as soon as I get them is a great way to improve my opening decisions and tighten up. Either way I make a very deliberate effort to always behave the same once I've looked at them. This means not only how I handle my cards, but where I put my hands, where I look with my eyes, and so on.

Learn New Ways to Put in Your Chips

It's extremely hard to notice if you've got a chip-handling tell for the simple reason that it will probably only appear when you're preoccupied with either a very strong hand or a bluff.

One way out of this is to decide ahead of time that for a given sit, you're going to always bet your chips in a certain way—neatly stacking and pushing them forward, say, or else splashing them. It may or may not be the way you usually handle your chips, but force yourself to follow this new rule for as long as you can. Eventually you'll catch yourself varying from this routine, and that's when you'll be able to notice if you've got a tell. If you become especially conscious in this area, you may even be able to generate false chip-handling tells. You can further free yourself from automatic habit by watching how other players bet their chips, and then copying them: some players toss them in with two hands, others roll them in, and so forth.

Look in an Imaginary Mirror

Mirrors aren't usually available at a live poker table, but you can still pretend that next to the table there's a mirror that reflects you perfectly. At some point during your sit, use your imagination to look into this mirror and see yourself honestly, as others are likely to see you. What does the mirror say about your clothes, your posture, your body language, your expression? How are opponents likely to read you based on this information?

Look in a Real Mirror; Record Yourself on Video

You may have heard of this trick elsewhere: if you play poker on the Internet as well as live, set up a mirror so you can glance at your reflection from time to time when you're engaged in a big hand. The idea is to catch any facial tells you may be displaying and not know about. Frankly, I've tried this and haven't found it helpful—I always seem to have the expression of a man looking in a mirror, and not much else. And I think that the expressions we permit ourselves when we know there's no audience are different from those we allow when in public. If you've been told that you have some obvious facial tells, however, it may be worth a try.

A better approach would be to arrange to record yourself on video. Probably the only place you could do this would be in a home game. I've never tried it myself, but if I played regularly for high stakes or in tournaments, I would. Following the same reasoning, I'm sure that top tournament players who appear on television regularly review their recorded appearances, both to spot tells they need to eliminate, and to possibly turn these tells into fake tells for the next tournament. There's too much money at stake for this not to be happening.

Pros and Cons of Wearing Shades

Countless players try to make themselves harder to read by wearing sunglasses. The question is, should you? My opinion is no. Sunglasses create several problems, including the following.

♣ In a dim cardroom, shades make it much harder to see the cards—not just your own cards, but the community cards, or even the cards all the way across the table if you're playing seven-card stud. They also make it harder to see your opponents, which means you'll be missing a lot of tells.

♣ One reason players wear sunglasses is to present an intimidating image. But if you're playing in a soft, loose cash game, the last thing you want to do is intimidate bad players into tightening up. And if by chance there are any truly tough players in the game, they may zero in on your need to be cool and use it against you. Either way, shades are usually a bad idea for regular play at a club or casino.

♣ Shades can seduce you into thinking that because your eyes are covered, you're not giving away any tells. What about your face, hands, and body? Better to throw away the shades and learn to control *all* of your anatomy, rather than rely on a crutch.

You'll notice that very few of the really famous tournament and cash game players wear shades. Those who do wear sunglasses include Phil Hellmuth Jr. and Chris Ferguson; those who don't include Annie Duke, her brother Howard Lederer, T. J. Cloutier, Doyle Brunson, Phil Ivey, Daniel Negreanu, Dan Harrington, Chip Reese, Gus Hansen, Barry Greenstein—shall I go on?

If you really feel the need to hide your eyes on occasion, you can wear a baseball cap with a long brim and duck your head when you want to. In my opinion, this is silly. If you only conceal your eyes during key points in a hand, aren't you creating yet another potential tell? And how can you study an opponent for tells if you're afraid to show your eyes?

Is All of This Really Worth It?

Finally, let's think a little more about the costs and benefits here. I think we agree that minimizing tells through consistent behavior is always a good thing. Beyond that, however, you need to be aware of the potential for diminishing returns. If you play mostly in low-limit games, your opponents won't notice the more subtle kinds of tells, so it doesn't pay to look for them in yourself. If, on the other hand, you play in tough games or big tournaments, it's a different story—now any extra effort is more likely to pay off.

Remember that when it comes to reverse tells, they'll again be most useful against clever, observant, thinking opponents, and least useful against the kind of loose-passive calling stations you run into at the low limits. So once again you've got a choice to make in rationing your efforts. As you go up in limits or enter progressively tougher tournaments, you'll soon encounter situations in which it becomes obvious after the fact that an opponent read you as clearly and easily as a billboard; that will be a warning signal to start improving yourself in this area.

Another thing to think about is that when it comes to deception against thinking opponents, there's a much more powerful tool available than reverse tells: varying your betting patterns. In fact, against tough opponents, you'll have no choice—you'll *have* to depart from optimum play on occasion. This is more important in no-limit than in limit, but even in limit, an occasional deceptive play is mandatory versus strong, aggressive players. Otherwise you just become too easy to read. For more on varying your play, I suggest the Sklansky classic, *The Theory of Poker*; if you specialize in no-limit hold'em in particular, you might also take a look at the two-volume set by Dan Harrington, *Harrington on Hold'em*.

CHAPTER 9

BEYOND TELLS: PROTECTING YOURSELF AGAINST ANGLE-SHOOTING

Reverse tells are attempts to deceive, and without deception, the game of poker would dry up like an old mud puddle. But some attempts to deceive fall outside the bounds of what's fair. These moves aren't always covered by the rules of poker, so they may not be clearly identifiable as cheating, but they're unethical nonetheless.

The general term for these kinds of cheap shots is "angle-shooting." Unlike tells, angles don't come up often enough to have a significant influence on your results—although once in a while they could cost you a big pot. So why are they important? First, if an angle *does* cost you a pot, it can ruin your mood and your session. Second, angle-shooters often target weaker players—those out to have a good time gambling. You want these sorts of players enjoying themselves and staying in your game, not being driven away by angle-shooters. Third, angle-shooting lives right next door to cheating, so letting it go unchecked can lead to even more egregious behavior.

In this chapter we'll run through some of the more common angles and explain how to guard against them. We'll also touch briefly upon certain outright forms of cheating, such as collusion between two players.

Marking the Boundary

To know what an angle is and isn't, we've got to first agree upon just when it is that deception goes too far. After all, many games feature not just bluffing or dissembling about hands in progress, but all kinds of banter, card-flashing, and other antics that in some eyes *might* constitute angle-shooting. Yet most players accept and even relish these goings-on.

The best criterion I know of for distinguishing acceptable from unacceptable deception comes courtesy of the late Andrew Glazer, in a nifty article he wrote on ethics in poker for *Card Player Magazine*. Essentially, Glazer's position is that it's perfectly ethical to deceive a player if the player isn't entitled to the information in question, but it's *not* ethical to deceive that player when he *is* entitled to the information.

For example, if you and I are betting and raising on the early streets in hold'em, it's okay for either one of us to claim we've got a flush, a full house, quads—whatever we want. That's because neither of us is entitled to see the other's hand yet. However, if we get to an actual showdown, the rules of most cardrooms say that the last bettor or raiser is required to show his cards first; the other players still in the hand have the option to show their cards next or muck; and after that the dealer awards the pot to the best hand.

But say you were the last bettor on the turn, and we've both checked the river. If you now declare, "I've got the flush" without showing your hand, in hopes I'll muck my own possibly winning hand, that's not a playful antic, that's an angle. You're attempting to deprive me of information I'm entitled to—namely, your cards face-up on the felt.

Other kinds of angle-shoots don't involve the withholding of information so much as "accidental" misrepresentations of the angle-shooter's intention. Usually this is in hopes of getting an opponent to do something differently than he normally would. An example would be raising out of turn to get a player who was about to bet to check instead.

Angle-shooters sometimes succeed with their ploys, but in almost every case it's because their victim has failed to take precautions. In the example I described, it should be ingrained deep in your psyche that you *never* let go of your hand at showdown until you've been shown a hand that you agree beats yours. This not only protects you against angle-shooting, but against unintentional misdeclares by other players and by the dealer.

Angle-shooting flourishes in low-limit public games and in home games, the former because that's where weak players congregate, and the latter because it's so easy to get away with in that setting. In a public game, if someone persists in angle-shooting despite requests to stop, you can ask the dealer to call the floor and have them warn the player—a prelude to ejection if necessary. In a home game, you'll have to police things yourself. Some home games are very good about this, but other home games are basically breeding grounds for cheaters.

You'll rarely see angle-shooting in a high-stakes games with serious players; even bad high-stakes players are usually sophisticated enough to protect themselves, and the tough players in such games won't tolerate anything that might irritate the whales upon whom they depend for their living. Not to mention it irritates them, too.

Common Angle-Shoots to Guard Against

This isn't a complete collection, but it does cover some of the most common angles. And from these, you'll get an idea of the kinds of situations and behaviors that constitute angle-shooting in general.

Angle: In hold'em, a player declares, "I've got the flush," when a third flush card hits the river. He's trying to get a better non-flush hand to muck, after which he'll flip up the "flush"—oops, it's two black or red cards, but of different suits! Gosh, he really thought he had it; too bad your hand is dead and he gets the pot.

What you should do: Hang on to your hand despite anything you hear an opponent say who hasn't shown his cards. Keep in mind, though, that we all misread our hands sometimes, so don't assume he was pulling an angle here and get rude.

Moreover, even if you *do* conclude he was angle-shooting, it's usually better not to accuse him of that in so many words. That can lead to pointless arguments that slow the game down and don't necessarily get the other players on your side. As with many angle-shots, it's better simply to ask that he stop doing it, without passing judgment on his motives. If he persists, you can take sterner measures, but until then, try to avoid putting him in a situation where he'll feel compelled to argue to save face.

Angle: At the river, there's been no bet. The angle-shooter hangs onto his hand while saying, "You win," hoping you'll muck prematurely, thinking the pot is safely yours. The moment you *do* muck, he flips over his cards and says, "Oh wait, I have Queen-high." By the rules of most cardrooms, he gets to take the pot down since your hand is dead.

What you should do: Hang on to your hand, hang on to your hand, hang on to your hand. Note that this stunt is far more explicit than the previous one. If a player pulls it even once, you can assume it was an angle-shoot and be careful in the future.

Angle: You go to bet, but as you're beginning your betting motion, a player behind you raises even though it's not his turn to act yet. Either you or the dealer object, and the player apologizes; but now, if you didn't want to get raised, you may check instead of betting. That's exactly what the angle-shooter is hoping for, since he wants a free card here.

What you should do: You can't assume it's an angle-shoot when he raises—it's not uncommon for a player to get excited and act out of turn. But if he then checks behind you, you'll know. You can't do anything about it this time, but at least you'll be on your guard.

Angle: Hiding cards in a community card game like hold'em so that other players don't know you're in the hand.

What you should do: Again, it's hard to know the first time this occurs whether it's deliberate; the natural tendency of some players is to over-guard their hands. Just ask the dealer to make sure everyone keeps his or her cards in sight, which is generally a requirement in card-rooms anyway.

Angle: Hiding chips or money behind your stack in a no-limit game so that opponents don't know how much you really have on the table. A variation on this involves hiding a stack of higher-value chips behind a stack or two of lower-value chips.

What you should do: Ask the dealer to make sure all the players keep all their chips visible.

Angle: You're first to act on the river, but even as you ponder whether to check or bet, your opponent flips over his cards as if the hand is already over. He's trying to keep you from betting—probably he'll claim he thought you checked.

What you should do: This usually only occurs when you're head-up. If your opponent has clearly acted out of turn, and you don't want to check it down, insist on your right to bet. Then go ahead and do so. Also, remember that in some no-limit cash games, a hand exposed before all the action is complete is dead; if so, ask the dealer to determine whether it applies in this case.

Angle: On the river, one player waves his hand in a vague gesture or mumbles something that sounds like "check," only to insist after the other player shows her hand that he didn't check and wants to bet. The angle-shooter here is hoping for a chance to steal the pot, but only if he sees that his opponent's hand is weak enough that she might not call a bet. Players who try this gimmick usually wait until the dealer is distracted.

What you should do: If the dealer allows the player to bet, call; often enough the angle-shooter's hand will be worse than yours. If it happens more than once, ask the dealer to call the floor simply to clarify the situation. The floor will rule one way or another; the point isn't so much to win the ruling as to put the spotlight on the offending player so he's less likely to angle-shoot on future hands.

Angle: Two buddies sitting at the same table have a habit of checking it down whenever they get head-up; their explanation is that since they're friends, they don't want to take each other's money. It seems harmless enough, and often is; but if experienced players are doing it, the potential is there for collusion. And collusion is more than angle-shooting—it's outright cheating.

Here's how it can work when it's not fully intentional: say these two buddies get involved in a three-way pot with another player. One or the other of the buddies is sure to realize that if he can drive this third player out early in the hand by putting in an extra raise with a hand that isn't really worth it, it'll be to his advantage. He and his buddy will then check it down at no additional cost. Regardless of whether he or his buddy wins at showdown, he's improved his chances of pocketing the third player's dead money.

If they're actively colluding, it gets even nastier. They'll execute plays like the one just described, but with an explicit agreement to split their winnings after the game. A favorite tactic involves signaling to each other whenever one of them catches a monster: if they can catch players in the middle, the two of them will put in raise after raise between them, even if the other buddy's hand is complete cheese. If this is what's happening, the buddy with the trash hand may quietly muck on the river, despite the fact he jammed every street before then.

By the way, this is why many cardrooms have a rule allowing any player who participated in a hand to ask to see the cards of all players at showdown; the point is to provide a way to expose collusion. The point is *not* to allow a player to gain strategic information any time he wants by seeing the winning player's cards. Some players abuse the rule that way, but you can always call the floor if they do it too often.

What you should do: If the two soft-playing buddies seem to be genuinely inexperienced, you can probably live and let live. But if they seem at all savvy, start watching for hands that follow one of the patterns I've described. If you suspect their act amounts to collusion, you could have the dealer call the floor so you can explain the situation. At the very least you'll be putting the entire table on alert. If the players didn't intend to cheat, they'll eventually calm down and maybe even apologize. If they *did* intend to cheat, you've spoiled their act. If you're not sure, another option is simply to move to another table.

The only bright side is that players who put this much effort into colluding often aren't very good, and they won't have much in the way of winnings to split anyway.

Other minor forms of angle-shooting include taking chips or money off the table (this is called "rat-holing," and isn't allowed by most cardrooms), abusing other players in hopes of putting them on tilt, bending cards (again, this is actually cheating), or gesturing with chips as if to raise a player who's about to bet (note that this is also a tell). Then there are the various ways of shorting the pot—in other words, putting in less than what's required. Three common angles here are splashing chips into the pot so they can't be easily counted, announcing a call but actually neglecting to put in the chips or cash when shown a winning hand, or quietly taking back any chips the dealer neglects to sweep into the pot.

In home games, an easy way to short the pot occurs when players who run out of chips during a hand are allowed to "go shy," using chips from the pot to keep track of how much they owe. If an angle-shooter goes shy, he'll conveniently forget to keep track of what he really owes—or even make a bet using chips he's just taken out of the pot for his shy! Given that going shy causes confusion even with honest players, I recommend banning the practice altogether. Simply require players to buy more chips if they run out during a hand.

CHAPTER 10

TALL TELL
STORIES

To round things out, here's a handful of anecdotes about tells. A number of these come from books I consider poker classics, even if they're not always instructional in nature.

Spanier's Sixth Sense

For the late poker writer David Spanier, the classification of tells by type and category probably would have spoiled his enjoyment of the game; his approach to the subject was purely romantic. If he read a player as weak, he asserted in his book *Total Poker*, it had nothing to do with logic or hand-reading and everything to do with instinct—a "sixth sense" that his opponent's show of strength was a façade.

"At that point all the mathematical calculations of odds and cards and money go out the window," Spanier wrote. "Which is not to say that theoretical formulae don't have their value, only that man cannot win by math alone."

A Non-Poker Tell

The value of involuntary tells was well-known long before poker became popular. A fictional example from the sea stories of author Patrick O'Brian, set during the early 1800s, has the spy Stephen Maturin watching the eyes of an opponent at the archaic game of whist—in particular, watching the man's pupils to see when they dilate, possibly indicating he's caught a good card.

How valid is this gimmick? In fact, the pupils typically *do* dilate when we're in the grip of strong emotion, according to researchers who've studied the autonomic nervous system. But the emotion itself could be anything from excitement to anxiety, so you'd have to know your victim quite well to guess which. You'd also need to have incredible eyesight to see so small a reaction under the artificial light common to casinos and clubs—either that, or be sitting within arm's reach of your target.

Sometimes Strong Means Strong

Not only are there reverse tells, there are even double reverse tells. A famous example comes from a no-limit hold'em hand between 1982 World Series of Poker champion Jack Strauss and an opponent who will remain nameless. Strauss was trailing, but when the river card hit, he crowed in delight before pushing in all his chips. His opponent called, relying on the following logic: if Strauss really had gotten lucky, he wouldn't have let it be known; instead, he'd have pretended to be weak. Therefore his show of delight was a reverse tell, attempting to steal the pot with a busted draw.

Alas, the call proved a mistake; Strauss had indeed caught his lucky card. He'd simply been behaving as he naturally would if he weren't a master poker player—in this case, the ultimate deception.

Crocodile Tears

How good is *Card Player Magazine* columnist Roy Cooke at reading tells? Pretty darn good. Here's a quick example from a column titled "Wrong Play, Right Results," from his book, *Real Poker II: The Play of Hands*.

Cooke has correctly folded a pair of deuces under the gun in a $40/$80 limit hold'em game. A local pro immediately to his left, stuck in what Cooke describes as "a desperate frame of mind," has limped in with what will later prove to be pocket Sixes. It's one of those wild California games that Cooke writes about so frequently, so it's no surprise that the pot is capped multiway before the flop, with the pro calling all three raises and reraises with his puny pocket pair.

Now the flop comes Q62, giving the pro a set, and here is where Cooke reads the man like a broken-spined book: "The local pro checked to the raisers, who bet and raised the pot to him. He hesitated, made a speech, and gave a reluctant call. I knew he held a big hand."

Cooke sees the hesitation, speech, and feigned reluctance for what they are—three tells in a row, all indicating the same thing—but his two opponents do not. They keep giving action, resulting in a nice pot for the pro on the river.

Caught Right-Handed

Herbert O. Yardley was a celebrated code-breaker for the United States during the 1920s and World War II, when he worked in China with the Nationalist movement. He was also a crack amateur poker player in his day, with a nearly photographic memory for dead cards and a conservative, odds-based approach to starting hands. His classic book, *The Education of a Poker Player*, combines his terse instructions for the correct play of games such as five-card stud and seven-card high-low with some of the most colorful anecdotes ever written about poker.

One of the best of these anecdotes concerns his early attempts to learn the game, when he was only 16 years old, at a saloon and poker club in his small hometown in Indiana during the early 1900s. The saloon was operated by James "Monty" Montgomery, a big, tough, intelligent Irishman in his midthirties, who also happened to be a far better player than most of the farmers and traveling salesmen who stopped by to gamble at five-card draw and other games.

The games were played "open," meaning players could bet not only the chips in front of them, but whatever money was in their pockets—or even their property or possessions—by signing IOUs. Moreover, the betting was what we would today call no-limit. The dangerous result was that conservative or weak players were apt to get bluffed out of their shirts, shoes, and homes.

Yardley's mother had just died, and his inheritance plus money saved from odd jobs gave him a stake of $200. Being a novice he played as tight as he dared, but even so his stake was whittled down to $50 within just a few days. He had only enough for one more try, after which he'd be flat broke.

He went to bed scared, and perhaps this was what prompted the nightmare that disrupted his sleep a few hours later. In it, Monty was pounding the poker table with his fist, yelling at some players who'd been arguing to shut up and deal. Yardley woke up sweating, wondering why the dream seemed so strangely significant.

Then he realized: Monty was left-handed, but in the dream he'd been pounding the table with his right hand.

And now Yardley remembered that in real life, Monty usually would bet holding his cards in his right hand and his chips in his left hand—but occasionally he'd do the reverse, shifting his cards to his left hand and using his right hand to throw his chips in. That was when he was bluffing—when he bet right-handed.

Armed with this knowledge, Yardley returned to the saloon the next day with his $50 short-stack, waited patiently until Monty bluffed at him, and unhesitatingly called with an unimproved pair of Aces, winning the pot. A few hands later, Monty bluffed right-handed again, but this time Yardley raised him—bluffing back with no hand at all. Monty folded, and once more Yardley raked in the pot, his hands trembling at his own audacity. Monty grumbled, but something about the kid must have struck him, for when the game broke shortly thereafter, he called Yardley into the back room and offered him a job as an assistant, helping to run the games.

Ungar's Instinct

Englishman Anthony Holden is a journalist and biographer —two of his subjects have been the Prince of Wales and Laurence Olivier—but he is also a poker fiend. Long before poker became as popular as it is today, he conceived the stunt of entering the World Series of Poker as a journalist and writing about his experience. It was part of a larger stunt of pretending for a full year that he was a professional poker player, when by any standards he was not.

In his book *Big Deal*, Holden notes that he actually made not one but two appearances in the World Series, finishing ignominiously both times. Both appearances had their moments, though, one of them being Holden's delicious confrontation with Stu Ungar, the champion from the previous year's event.

Blind chance finds Ungar and Holden seated at the same starting table, and a further quirk of luck sees Holden getting AT of Spades as his hole cards on his very first hand. Holden limps in early position, several other limpers follow, before Ungar in the big blind puts in a raise. On one of those wild English whims Holden decides Ungar is just trying to steal, and reraises. Everyone folds around to Ungar, who looks at Holden "sulkily" before putting in a third raise, the biggest yet.

Oops. Too late Holden realizes Ungar actually has a hand, probably a biggish pocket pair. Holden calls, but things look dim for the biographer. Then the dealer lays out the flop, and the third card rolls off the deck in the form of "a beautiful, shiny red Ace."

Ungar checks, and there now occur two fairly dramatic tells. The first is when Holden goes to bet, and realizes to his dismay that his hands are trembling. The second tell comes from Ungar: "[My bet] seemed to have an almost physical impact on Ungar, who hit the back of his chair as if invisibly socked on the jaw, and stared moodily at the flop."

So much for poker being a game of concealed information. Snarling, Ungar mucks his hand, and Holden goes on to—well, to get busted out midway through the tournament, but that's another story.

Shot by His Own Angle

In his classic *Super/System*, Doyle Brunson recounts an especially egregious attempt at angle-shooting—one that backfires badly on the angle-shooter when his target catches on.

A player identified only as "the kid" by Brunson has just taken a seat in Brunson's regular game of no-limit Ace-to-Five lowball. Even if you've never played lowball, you can guess by the name of the game that the best low wins—in this case, a wheel, since straights and flushes don't count against the low. This is a nasty game when played no-limit, and it gets even nastier when the deck includes a single Joker, playable as a wild card.

The kid is unfamiliar with lowball, so the players have to explain it to him. The Joker in particular confuses the kid, and he asks what it's for. At this point a particularly impatient regular, whom Brunson chooses to call Grumpy for the purposes of this anecdote, decides he's had enough. The Joker can be used for anything you want, he barks. "Now will someone *deal* for God's sake?"

In fact, Grumpy's instructions are not quite correct. In this variant of lowball, you're usually *not* allowed to make the Joker whatever you please—instead, it's counted as the lowest possible card in your hand toward a low hand. A few hands later, Grumpy and the kid get head-up in a small pot. At showdown, Grumpy demands to know what the kid has.

"I've got an Eight," the kid announces, spreading 4567 with the Joker.

Accustomed to high-only poker, the kid has misdeclared his hand. But rather than correct him by pointing out that the Joker in this case plays as an Ace, giving him a Seven-low, Grumpy gleefully announces he too has an Eight-low, only it's better—a 23678. With a cackle he takes the pot. The other players don't say anything since they're not in the hand, but there's a general feeling of disapproval in the air. Grumpy is oblivious.

The kid isn't as dumb as Grumpy takes him for. He sits there and thinks, and stews, and thinks, and then his face reddens as he realizes how he was taken. A few hands later he and Grumpy get in another pot, only this time it becomes huge, with Grumpy putting the kid all-in for about $400 after the draw.

Key to understanding the action at this point is an additional wrinkle in the rules: a player who draws a pat Seven or better isn't allowed to check. After the draw, the kid in fact *did* check, so Grumpy can be assured the kid has no better than an Eight-low—if that.

Even better, from Grumpy's point of view, is that he himself holds the second-best possible Eight, A2358; in the jargon this is known as an Eight-Five. The kid needs an Eight-Four to beat him, Grumpy gloatingly announces, spreading his cards on the felt.

Isn't that interesting, the kid says—he just happens to *have* an Eight-Four. And with that he shows A234-Joker.

"That's a *wheel*, not an Eight-four—and you can't check a wheel, sonny!" Grumpy says, and hoots in triumph. Under the rules, he's entitled to take back his all-in bet, and he begins to reach for his $400. But the kid stops him. If he could use the Joker for an Eight before, as Grumpy allowed him to do, he can use it for an Eight now, right?

Caught in a trap of his own making, Grumpy tries to argue his way out of it, but the other players don't want to hear it. The kid takes the pot, leaving Grumpy to contemplate the wages of angle-shooting sin.

A Mother's Smile

James A. McKenna is a practicing therapist, poker buff, and author of a book on poker psychology, *Beyond Tells: Power Poker Psychology*. Most of the book is about reading players and yourself through an analysis of various attitudes and habits, including "life scripts" which betray deeper psychological issues. But McKenna also talks to some extent about tells, and at one point he describes a tell of his own—one whose origin dates all the way back to childhood.

It seems that whenever McKenna fibbed to his mother, he'd look her directly in the eyes, daring her to call him a liar. Naturally she caught on, and it came to the point that she'd only believe him when he *didn't* make a special effort to look her in the eye.

Later, as an adult, McKenna resorted to this same ruse when bluffing: he'd stare the other player in the eye. But he never realized that good players were seeing through him until one particular player smiled at him. As McKenna says, "Immediately, I remembered the smile on Mom's face when she'd said, 'I'll always know where you're not telling the truth, Jimmy.'"

Like Proust's madeleine cookie dipped in a cup of tea, that fragment of memory was all it took to change McKenna's life forever (well, his poker life, anyway). From then on, he turned his tell to his advantage. He'd set an initial pattern of looking his opponent in the eye while bluffing. Then, when his opponent caught on, he'd switch, and look his opponent in the eye when *not* bluffing—and so on, and so on.

Finding Your Hand on the Ceiling

There exists an older class of poker instructional books than the highly technical ones authored today. In this older, gentler world, one prolific author in particular was A. D. Livingston, who wrote a number of books for home poker players in the 1970s. (He also wrote an article for *Life* magazine in 1968 titled "Hold Me: A Wild New Poker Game, and How to Tame It." Yes, that was indeed Texas hold'em he was writing about, back in an era so foggy even the name was different.)

In one book, *Poker Strategy and Winning Play*, Livingston lists 13 different tells to watch for, including verbal tells, loading up on chips, and so on. He also relates his favorite poker story, one involving a player's individual tell. It goes as follows.

The game was $2 limit, played in the back of a pool hall. The tightest player in this little group was an old fellow who was so short he had to sit on a stool instead of a chair to reach the table; his understandable if unkind nickname was Runt.

His particular tell, which had obviously become well-known in the game, was to rear back on his stool and stare at the ceiling whenever he made a big hand. To accentuate the maneuver, he'd scratch his chin as if in deep thought. Then he'd act as if he was being forced to put in a little raise.

During one particular game of five-card stud, Runt caught a King on the fourth and final upcard. An opponent, the owner of the pool hall, bet out with wired Jacks that he'd had all along. Runt looked at his King, rechecked his hole card, and reared back per usual. Of course, he'd made a pair of Kings, giving him the best hand. Now he had to pretend he was thinking about it.

Since Runt was busy staring at the ceiling, he didn't notice his opponent quickly and deftly switching his hole card with Runt's. At length, Runt's eyes came down and he drawled out his raise. Of course he was called. He went to triumphantly flip over his King in the hole, and his eyes bugged out: he had a red Jack in the hole, not a King after all.

"I've been screwed," Runt blurted out, according to Livingston, "and there ain't a man in the house that I can whup!"

Being a good sport, the owner of the pool hall then switched the cards back and awarded the pot to Runt—at least in the story.

Sound Familiar?

Mike Caro's *Book of Tells* isn't the only book to focus on draw poker—there are others, including the out-of-print classic *Play Poker, Quit Work, and Sleep Till Noon* by John Fox and a hefty tome by Mason Malmuth somewhat more prosaically titled *Winning Concepts in Draw and Lowball.*

As the head of Two Plus Two Publishing, Malmuth has helped fuel the poker boom by coauthoring or publishing a long string of highly regarded instructional books on hold'em, stud, tournament play, and poker in general. By comparison, *Winning Concepts* is probably on no one's reading list these days, given the relative antiquity of the games involved. (Yes, triple-draw lowball is apparently a fad at the high limits, but that's not the kind of lowball Malmuth was writing about.) In a way it's a shame, for the book has a lot of interesting if highly technical information, some of which might be applied to other poker games with a little imagination.

Take the chapter titled "Table Talk." In it, Malmuth lists 16 different verbal tells and what they usually signify. Even though Malmuth was writing about draw and lowball, the phrases he captured here still sound strangely familiar—for the simple reason that players repeat them to this very day in games including seven-card stud and hold'em. Here's just a short selection, without Malmuth's accompanying explanations—see how many you recognize.

"Loose call." "I have to bet." "Someone's got to open." "What, no callers?" "I know you have trips." "Just to keep the others out."

And yes, even the old chestnut, "Give me a Heart."

Some Things Can't Be Learned

Another book on poker psychology, this one by Alan Schoonmaker, is titled (what else?) *The Psychology of Poker*. Like James McKenna, author of *Beyond Tells*, Schoonmaker spends much of his time discussing how players can be read by personality type, underlying motivations, and so on. But he, too, takes some time out to talk about tells. He endorses this form of reading opponents—particularly if you can spot and record individual tells, which he believes are more reliable than generic tells.

What Schoonmaker *doesn't* endorse, however, is the notion that we can all grow our intuition and people-reading ability to be on par with that of a poker genius like Doyle Brunson. He notes that in *Super/System* Brunson instructs his readers to judge whether a player is bluffing based in part on "feel." Says Schoonmaker in response: "That sort of advice is as silly as telling a young basketball player that he should develop Michael Jordan's reflexes. Those reflexes are a gift that he will never have."

Schoonmaker notes that even after studying psychology for many years, he's still amazed at the depth of some people's intuition when compared to his own. As an example, he relates that he once worked with someone for months—and yet his wife told him, after meeting the man for just two minutes, that the man was a crook and shouldn't be trusted.

His wife turned out to be right, Schoonmaker says—but she could never tell him how she knew, only that she just knew.

Cracking the Code

Peter O. Steiner began playing poker seriously during World War II as an officer on board the aircraft carrier USS *Independence*. He kept going with what he describes as "a profitable hobby" in the decades thereafter, during a lengthy career as a professor of economics at various universities. After he retired, he decided the world needed a grown-up book about amateur poker and that he would write it. The resulting *Thursday Night Poker* is an enjoyable read, especially for Steiner's refreshing honesty about just why so many adults gather each week at one or another's home to play poker—and no, it's not to "maximize" their "hourly rate," regardless of what other poker books today may tell you.

Steiner has a number of wry anecdotes in the book, including one in which he relates how very early in his poker apprenticeship, he learned to make use of a highly unusual tell.

He was playing in a game on board a Navy ship; the game happened to include two Air Force officers along for an eight-day voyage. The game of choice was high-low seven-card stud. Steiner soon realized the two Air Force officers shared a bizarre approach to betting. Instead of betting and raising normal amounts, like $10 or $20, they'd always bet or raise unusual amounts, like $23, $39, and so on. As befits a future economics professor, it didn't take Steiner long to realize what was going on. To start with, the two officers were cheating by signaling to each other whether they intended to go high or low by betting an odd number when going low and an even number when going high.

If that had been all, Steiner might not have caught on. But the colluders made the mistake of further adjusting their bets by grading their holdings. For example, an amount ending in a 1 or a 3 would signal a very good low hand, while an amount ending in a 7 or 9 would signal a weak low hand.

By the third day of the voyage, Steiner had cracked the code and was using it like a tell against the two officers. The result was highly profitable, he writes—in fact, "It ended up paying for my first automobile."

POKER
GLOSSARY

all-in. To make or call a bet with all the money you have on the table. Common in *no-limit*, much less so in *low limit*.

angle-shooting. Unethical attempts to deceive naïve players into throwing away their hands, failing to bet when they should, or otherwise making mistakes that benefit the angle-shooter. A typical play would be to raise out of turn as a player bets, hoping to scare the bettor into checking. The angle-shooter can now check behind and take the free card he was looking for.

ante. A preset amount placed in the pot by each player before each hand, to induce action. See also *blinds*.

baby. A small card such as a Six or lower, or a flush or straight headed by such a small card.

backdoor. In hold'em, making a hand by virtue of catching required cards on both the turn and the river. An example would be a backdoor flush where you catch your fourth and fifth flush cards on the turn and river.

bad beat. Losing to a much weaker hand that not only got lucky and outdrew you, but that a sensible player would have folded early on given the poor odds.

bankroll. Working capital dedicated completely to poker. Many recreational players don't have a bankroll as such, but all successful professionals do.

betting pattern. A player's habitual sequence of checks, bets, or raises when holding a given hand in a given situation. Great players focus on reading betting patterns even more than they do on reading tells.

big blind. In hold'em and Omaha, the player who posts the larger of the two *blinds* prior to cards being dealt. In *limit* hold'em, this blind is usually the same size as the initial bet before the flop and on the flop. The big blind sits two seats to the left of whomever the dealer is for the hand.

blank. An upcard that appears unlikely to improve a player's hand.

blinds. Blind bets posted by designated players; used in place of the *ante* for games including lowball and hold'em. The blinds rotate around the table with each new hand. See also *small blind* and *big blind*.

board. In community card games, the common upcards used by all players; in games like seven-card stud, the individual upcards for each player.

Broadway. The highest possible straight, from Ten to Ace.

button. In hold'em, the player whose position gives her the privilege of acting last on the flop and thereafter; symbolized in live play by a plastic dealer button.

calling station. A player who routinely calls bets or raises all the way to the river with weak hands, or sometimes with no hand at all.

cash game. As opposed to a tournament, a game played for cash rather than for prize money.

crying call. Calling when you feel you're most likely beat, but the odds mandate you attempt to see the showdown. Crying calls are most common when the pot is big or you're up against a player who bluffs frequently.

cutoff. In hold'em, the player directly in front of the *button*. A crucial position because if the cutoff raises before the flop, he may be able to knock the button out and thereby acquire the privilege of being last to act on later *streets*. An open-raise from this position may not only knock out the button but steal the *blinds*, ending the hand right there.

dead button. In hold'em, a situation where the player who would have inherited the dealer *button* in this hand has gotten up from the table. Different cardrooms have different rules for handling a dead button; some allow the button to stop at the unoccupied seat for that hand, while others require that the button move forward to the next player present.

dealer. See *button*.

door card. In seven-card stud, the third card or upcard dealt to all players in the hand.

draw out. To win by completing a drawing hand—for example, catching a card on the river to make your straight and beat a player holding top pair.

expectation. A term borrowed from mathematics to express the likelihood that a given poker decision will make you money in the long run.

flop. In games such as hold'em and Omaha, the dealing of the first three community cards. See also *river*.

gutshot. An inside straight draw.

head-up. A hand involving only two players. Also called "heads-up."

implied odds. Odds that compare the price of calling a relatively small bet now with the chances of winning a big pot later on, should your hand improve. Drawing hands usually require implied odds to have positive *expectation*. See also *pot odds*.

kicker. The highest unpaired card in a player's hand. For example, in hold'em, if your hole cards are AK and the flop comes with an Ace, you have flopped top pair with your Ace and hold the best possible kicker with your King.

limit. A betting structure in which bets are restricted to preset amounts; in contrast to *no-limit*.

limper. In community card games like hold'em, a *limper* is any player who enters a pot before the flop by merely calling the amount of the *big blind*, rather than raising. This is called "limping" or "limping in."

little blind. See *small blind*.

lock. A hand that can't be beaten, no matter how many more cards are dealt. An example would be making a royal flush on the turn in hold'em: no matter which card comes on the river—even if the board pairs and gives another player *quads*—this hand is a lock. The lock is a superior version of the *nuts* since the nuts refers merely to the best possible hand so far.

loose-aggressive. Said of a player who not only tends to play a lot of hands, but plays them aggressively, betting and raising fairly more than usual. See also *loose-passive*.

loose-passive. Said of a player who tends to play a lot of hands, but only bets or raises with extremely strong hands. See *calling station*.

low limit. *Limit* poker played for small stakes, typically anywhere from $2/$4 to $10/$20. In this notation, the amount before the slash indicates the bet size on early streets, while the amount after the slash indicates the bet size on later streets.

maniac. A player prone to betting and raising wildly.

muck. To fold or discard your hand by tossing it face-down in the direction of the dealer, who then gathers up the cards. A mucked hand is a dead hand and cannot win a pot, even if it was the best hand before it was folded.

multiway. A hand involving more than two players. See also *head-up*.

no-limit. A betting structure in which a player can bet all of his money at any point in the hand.

nuts. The best possible hand on any given *street*, given the available information. The nuts can and frequently does change as more cards are dealt. For example, on a flop of J♦T♦Q♥ in hold'em, the nuts is a Broadway straight; but if the turn comes the 3♦, it's now an Ace-high flush; and if the river comes the K♦, it's now a royal flush.

outs. The number of unseen cards remaining in the deck that can theoretically make you the winning hand.

overpair. In hold'em, a pocket pair larger than any pair made possible by the *board*.

pot odds. The ratio between the amount in the pot and the size of the bet you have to call to continue in the hand. Good players compare pot odds to their chances of winning to decide whether a given action will be profitable in the long run. See also *implied odds*.

quads. Four of a kind.

ragged. Said of a *board* when the cards aren't close together in rank or suit. For example, a ragged flop in hold'em might be J72.

rags. Several cards that together seem to have little value in making a hand. See also *ragged, blank*.

rainbow. In community card games like hold'em, a flop of all different suits.

rake. In public poker, the house's share of each pot, generally collected after the hand is over. Low limits sometimes have rakes as high as 10 percent.

reverse tell. A false or fake *tell* generated by a player who hopes to fool an observant opponent. For example, a player may cover her mouth as if she were bluffing when in fact she has a strong hand.

river. The final *street* in all forms of poker. See also *flop* and *turn*.

rock. A very tight, conservative player.

rolled up. In seven-card stud, to be dealt three of a kind, or *trips*, on your first three cards.

runner-runner. In hold'em, catching critical cards on both the turn and river to complete a draw.

running bad. In the middle of a long streak of bad cards or bad beats.

short stack. Few chips left with which to play. Most meaningful in tournament play, where rising blinds and antes threaten to devour short stacks.

slowplay. To merely call or even check with a very strong hand early in a hand in hopes of trapping weaker hands for large bets later on.

small blind. In hold'em and Omaha, the player who posts the smaller of the two *blinds*, generally from one-third to two-thirds the amount of the big blind. The small blind sits immediately to the left of whoever the dealer is for the hand.

spike. To catch a lucky card.

split pair. Used exclusively in stud; refers to a starting hand in which your doorcard makes a pair with one of your down cards. For example, if your doorcard is an Ace and you've got an Ace and a Three in the pocket, you've got split Aces. See also *wired pair*.

spread limit. A form of *limit* poker in which the bet size can vary within a given range, rather than being fixed as an absolute amount. For example, in a $1-$5 spread limit, the initial bet can be anywhere between $1 and $5.

steam. To get angry, usually as a result of some misfortune at the table, and start playing badly.

streets. The stages of a poker hand according to how many cards have been dealt. For example, in seven-card stud, Third Street occurs when the first three starting cards have been dealt; the streets that follow in that game are Fourth, Fifth, Sixth, and Seventh. The final street in all games is also known as the *river*.

string raise. A raise in which the player puts forward enough chips to call a bet, then brings forward additional chips with which to raise. Prohibited by nearly all cardrooms, but frequently seen in relaxed home games.

suck out. See *draw out*.

table stakes. The usual convention for all poker these days. A player can't bet money that isn't already on the table at the start of the deal, nor can he be raised out of a pot by a bet larger than that amount. In the latter

179

situation, he is allowed to call *all-in* with his remaining money.

tell. A gesture, facial expression, change in posture, or other unintentional signal that gives away the strength or weakness of a player's hand. See also *reverse tell*.

trip up. In seven-card stud, to make three of a kind by catching a third card of the rank of your starting pair.

trips. Three of a kind.

turn. In games such as hold'em and Omaha, the dealing of the fourth community card. See also *flop* and *river*.

value bet. To bet your hand on the river when you think it is likely to be the best hand by a relatively small margin. Usually applies to limit poker rather than no-limit.

variance. A mathematical term referring to the long-term ups and downs of your poker *bankroll*.

wheel. The lowest possible straight, from Ace to Five.

wired pair. Used exclusively in stud; refers to a starting hand in which your two down cards make up a pair, with an upcard of a different rank. See also *split pair*.

FURTHER RESOURCES

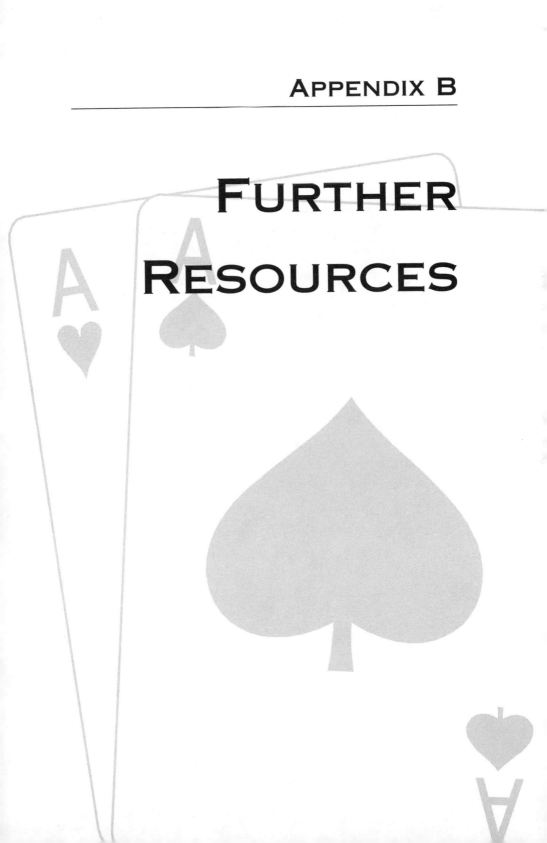

Other Books about Tells

Caro, Mike. *Caro's Book of Poker Tells*. New York: Cardoza
    Publishing, 2003.

We've got a category of one here because, as of this
writing, this is the only other book on the market devoted
solely to tells. First published in 1984 as *The Book of Tells*,
Caro's masterpiece keeps getting reprinted under different titles and publishers. The tells for draw poker aren't
much use anymore, but those for seven-card stud and
hold'em are as valid as ever. And the photographs are both
instructional and a lot of fun.

Books about Poker Fundamentals

As I've stressed throughout this text, tells won't help you
if your game isn't strong. If you're a beginner or intermediate player, the following books are the best for learning
both no-limit and limit hold'em, as well as seven-card
stud.

Brunson, Doyle, et al. *Doyle Brunson's Super System: A
    Course in Power Poker*. New York: Cardoza Publishing,
    1979.

This is a retitled reprint of the famous silver-backed volume
that Brunson initially self-published as *How I Made over
$1,000,000 Playing Poker*. Perhaps that sounded gratuitous,
for Brunson soon renamed the book *Super/System*—a title I
prefer for its aberrant punctuation, in keeping with the
other emphatic violations of punctuation and typography

that bring the text to fire-breathing life. If you remember the opening scene of *Rounders*, Mike McDermott keeps part of his bankroll hidden in a hollowed-out copy of *Super/System* in a twisted form of homage that implies he's so thoroughly absorbed the material that he can desecrate it.

Along with other seminal works, *Super/System* revolutionized poker by giving away information previously restricted to professionals. If you enjoy poker at all, you can't *not* read this book. It's tremendous fun, and Brunson's key insights are still valid, even for recreational players. On the other hand, much of the game-specific information is so dated as to be questionable.

In particular, the chapter on no-limit is priceless but treacherous: you can't push around no-limit games the way Brunson used to. Everybody these days plays small suited connectors (often badly, but that's another matter), and the small games you're likely to start in reward peddling the nuts far more than they do Brunson-style bluffing. Where the chapter still shines is in the detailed advice on how to play different kinds of hands depending on the board, the opponent, and the action.

* * *

Burgess, Randy, and Carl Baldassarre. *The Pocket Idiot's Guide to Texas Hold'em*. New York: Alpha Books, 2005.

This book is primarily for beginners. It focuses mostly on limit hold'em but covers the basics of no-limit as well. Unlike most other beginner books, we introduce you to key concepts you'll need later on, such as implied odds, pot equity, and more.

* * *

Harrington, Dan, and Bill Robertie. *Harrington on Hold'em, Volume I: Strategic Play*. Henderson, NV: Two Plus Two Publishing, 2004.

———. *Harrington on Hold'em, Volume II: The End Game*. Henderson, NV: Two Plus Two Publishing, 2004.

This two-volume set for no-limit tournament play is not for beginners but is vital reading for intermediate players. It contains useful information for cash games as well, though you have to make some mental adjustments.

* * *

Miller, Ed, with David Sklansky and Mason Malmuth. *Small Stakes Hold'em: Winning Big with Expert Play*. Henderson, NV: Two Plus Two Publishing, 2004.

About limit hold'em only, this book has become an instant classic among smart young players seeking to exploit the hold'em boom, and with good reason. Move on to it as soon as you have even a few months of playing experience under your belt.

* * *

Reuben, Stewart, and Bob Ciaffone. *Pot-Limit and No-Limit Poker*. Saginaw, MI: Bob Ciaffone, 1999.

This is the essential book for anyone getting started in pot-limit and no-limit. It's doubly vital if you started your poker career with limit and are now switching over to no-limit; playing no-limit as if it were limit is a catastrophe, and this book can save you from that.

* * *

Sklansky, David. *The Theory of Poker*. Henderson, NV: Two Plus Two Publishing, 1994.

This book is vital for anyone playing limit poker; it's slightly less useful for no-limit, but still important. For beginners it will seem difficult reading at first, but it's like a fine if slightly crabby wine: it keeps getting better every time you go back to it.

* * *

Sklansky, David, and Mason Malmuth. *Hold'em Poker for Advanced Players*. Henderson, NV: Two Plus Two Publishing, 1999.

This used to be the classic work on limit hold'em for players just past the beginner level, but it's since been replaced for low-limit play by the Ed Miller book. For preparation for high-limit games it remains a must.

* * *

Sklansky, David, Mason Malmuth, and Ray Zee. *Seven-Card Stud for Advanced Players*. Henderson, NV: Two Plus Two Publishing, 1999.

The only stud book to read if you want to move up to the middle and high limits.

* * *

West, Roy. *7-Card Stud: 42 Lessons How to Win at Medium and Lower Limits*. New York: Cardoza Publishing, 2004.

A beginner's reference for limit seven-card stud first published in 1996, West's book remains by far the best of its kind. Ignore the spate of more recent but inferior stud books. West's two key points are to play intelligently tight (watch for dead cards) and to read your opponents' betting patterns. This is the book that first taught me how to win at poker.

Exercises for Improving Tell-Reading Ability

Austin, Miriam, and Barry Kaplan. *Meditation for Wimps: Finding Your Balance in an Imperfect World*. New York: Sterling Publishing, 2003.

As with yoga, you can buy any number of books on meditation. This one is particularly nice because of its agnostic attitude. The truth is, though, you don't have to be a Buddhist to benefit from Buddhist-influenced meditation techniques such as those described in this book.

These Buddhist forms of meditation, usually labeled in English as insight meditation, are, in my opinion, more useful for serious poker players than other New Age or Westernized forms of meditation, such as Transcendental

Meditation or the so-called "relaxation response" popularized by Herbert Benson. Insight meditation goes well beyond simple relaxation; if you stay with it, it will teach you emotional liberation *and* emotional self-control at the same time, a very neat trick. And remember, experienced Buddhist meditators have scored highly on tests of reading micro expressions.

* * *

Kraftsow, Gary. *Yoga for Wellness: Healing with the Timeless Teachings of Viniyoga*. New York: Penguin, 1999.

Actually, any good yoga book will do; I happen to like this one because of its emphasis on safe postures and healing. Yoga will teach not only relaxation, but the self-composure that so many poker players lack at the table. It's also a good way to learn better breathing. Although a book is helpful as a reference, start with a class to get the idea.

* * *

Weil, Dr. Andrew. *Natural Health, Natural Medicine: The Complete Guide to Wellness and Self-Care for Optimum Health*. Boston: Houghton Mifflin, revised edition 2004.

If you're like most Americans, you probably have bad breathing habits and don't know it. The chapter in this book titled "Preventive Maintenance" includes excellent descriptions of easy-to-learn breathing exercises for both relaxation and energy. I use these exercises at the poker table, and they really help—not only for helping me relax to spot more tells, but for better decision making in general.

* * *

Dimitrius, Jo-Ellan, and Mark C. Mazzarella. *Reading People: How to Understand People and Predict Their Behavior—Anytime, Anyplace.* New York: Ballantine Books, 1999.

Although I referenced this work in chapter 7, I don't consider it a must-read for the poker buff—Dimitrius's primary experience is with courtrooms, not cardrooms, and you'll have to do some creative thinking if you want to adopt her tips for use at the table. But the book is interesting overall, especially for students of human behavior.

More about Micro Expressions

Speaking of micro expressions, you can learn more about Paul Ekman's research by visiting his website at www.paulekman.com. Several articles are available as free PDF downloads. These are written for academic audiences, but still serve as a good introduction to his research.

If you're interested in ordering the CD-ROM that teaches how to read micro expressions, click the Training CD link on the website. I consider this a must-have for the serious high-stakes or tournament player who's weak on reading facial expressions.

Ekman has written a number of books about emotions, micro emotions, and the face. By far the most accessible is *Emotions Revealed* (Owl Books, 2004). You can order it directly from Ekman's website or from any bookseller.

Notes

Chapter 1

"In his prime, Doyle Brunson was perhaps the most feared no-limit hold'em player alive . . ." Brunson, Doyle, et al., *Doyle Brunson's Super System: A Course in Power Poker*. New York: Cardoza Publishing, 1979.

"Tournament pro Daniel Negreanu puts it this way, writing in *Card Player Magazine* . . ." Negreanu, Daniel, "The Truth About Tells," *Card Player Magazine* 16, no. 15, 2003.

"'He looked stiff. Very stiff.'" Negreanu, Daniel, "My Back's Against the Wall," *Full Contact Poker*, December 15, 2004, http://www.fullcontactpoker.com/poker-journal.php ?subaction=showfull&id=1103101990&archive=&start_ from=&ucat=1& (accessed November 6, 2005).

"According to Cooke, reading Mike Caro's *Book of Tells* early on sensitized him to the idea of tells . . ." Cooke, Roy, "Reading More Than Tells!," *Card Player Magazine* 15, no. 6, 2002.

"Mason Malmuth, a well-known poker writer, has written that tells were such a big part of draw . . ." Malmuth, Mason, *Poker Essays, Volume II*. Henderson, NV: Two Plus Two Publishing, 1996.

Chapter 2

"... Doyle Brunson mentions it in his classic book *Super/System* ..." Brunson, Doyle, *Doyle Brunson's Super System: A Course in Power Poker.* New York: Cardoza Publishing, 1979.

"... in his introduction, Caro elucidates what he calls his Great Law of Tells ..." Caro, Mike, *Caro's Book of Poker Tells.* New York: Cardoza Publishing, 2003.

"Brunson writes that on occasion, he'd repeat a phrase like 'Gee whiz' every time he bluffed ..." Brunson, Doyle, *Doyle Brunson's Super System: A Course in Power Poker.* New York: Cardoza Publishing, 1979.

"As Ciaffone notes, it's easy to keep a poker face ..." Ciaffone, Robert, and Stewart Reuben, *Pot-Limit & No-Limit Poker.* Saginaw, MI: Bob Ciaffone, 1999.

Chapter 3

"... I've just read in Mike Caro's *Book of Tells* that Asians at the poker table ..." Caro, Mike, *Caro's Book of Poker Tells.* New York: Cardoza Publishing, 2003.

"So says poker writer Bob Ciaffone, who ought to know, being in his midsixties himself ..." Ciaffone, Bob, *Improve Your Poker.* Saginaw, MI: Bob Ciaffone, 1997.

Chapter 7

"What we call intuition is nearly always the surfacing of a submerged memory, a barely noticed event, or some combination of the two." Dimitrius, Jo-Ellan, and Mark C. Mazzarella, *Reading People: How to Understand People and Predict Their Behavior—Anytime, Anyplace.* New York: Ballantine Books, 1999.

"Among this skilled minority, Ekman reports . . ." Ekman, Paul, Maureen O'Sullivan, and Mark G. Frank, "A Few Can Catch a Liar," *Psychological Science* 10, no. 3, 1999. Also Boyce, Barry, "Two Sciences of Mind," *Shambhala Sun*, September 2005.

Chapter 8

". . . listening to a tape recorder to tell him when to bet or raise . . ." Hayano, David, *Poker Faces.* Berkeley, CA: University of California Press, 1983.

"Doyle Brunson has written that during a big hand, he'd refuse to let anyone engage him in conversation . . ." Brunson, Doyle, *Doyle Brunson's Super System: A Course in Power Poker.* New York: Cardoza Publishing, 1979.

Chapter 10

"If he read a player as weak, he asserted in his book *Total Poker* . . ." Spanier, David, *Total Poker.* Harpenden, U.K.: High Stakes Publishing, 2002.

"A fictional example from the sea stories of author Patrick O'Brian . . ." O'Brian, Patrick, *Treason's Harbour.* New York: W.W. Norton & Co., 1992.

"Strauss was trailing, but when the river card hit . . ." Alvarez, A., *The Biggest Game in Town*. San Francisco: Chronicle Books, 2002.

"Cooke has correctly folded a pair of deuces under the gun . . ." Cooke Jr., Roy, *Real Poker II: The Play of the Hands*. Inglewood, CA: Mike Caro University, 2001.

"Herbert O. Yardley was a celebrated code-breaker for the United States . . ." Yardley, Herbert O., *The Education of a Poker Player*. Athens, GA: Orloff Press, 1998.

"Englishman Anthony Holden is a journalist and biographer . . ." Holden, Anthony, *Big Deal: One Year as a Professional Poker Player*. Kent, U.K.: Abacus Press, 2002.

"In his classic *Super/System*, Doyle Brunson recounts . . ." Brunson, Doyle, *Doyle Brunson's Super System: A Course in Power Poker*. New York: Cardoza Publishing, 1979.

"James A. McKenna is a practicing therapist, poker buff, and author . . ." McKenna, James A., *Beyond Tells: Power Poker Psychology*. New York: Citadel Press, 2005.

"In one book, *Poker Strategy and Winning Play*, Livingston lists 13 different tells . . ." Livingston, A.D., *Poker Strategy and Winning Play*. Woodstock, NY: Lyons Press, 2000.

". . . a hefty tome by Mason Malmuth . . ." Malmuth, Mason, *Winning Concepts in Draw and Lowball*. Henderson, NV: Two Plus Two Publishing, 1987.

"Another book on poker psychology, this one by Alan Schoonmaker . . ." Schoonmaker, Alan, *The Psychology of Poker*. Henderson, NV: Two Plus Two Publishing, 2000.

"After he retired, he decided the world needed a grown-up book about amateur poker . . ." Steiner, Peter O., *Thursday-Night Poker: How to Understand, Enjoy—and Win*. New York: Ballantine Books, 2005.

ABOUT THE AUTHORS

Randy Burgess is a freelance author, book doctor, and writing consultant. He has also been a newspaper reporter, and his first introduction to poker came in the form of home games with fellow reporters. Two decades later, his favorite cash game is no-limit hold'em. Other poker books Randy has written include *Stepping Up: The Recreational Player's Guide to Winning Casino Poker* and, as coauthor with Carl Baldassarre, *The Pocket Idiot's Guide to Texas Hold'em.* He lives in Woodstock, New York.

Carl Baldassarre is an author and advertising copywriter; currently he's also a creative supervisor at the OgilvyOne advertising agency in New York City. Carl contributed to both of Randy's prior poker books, supplying material on seven-card stud to *Stepping Up* and coauthoring *The Pocket Idiot's Guide to Texas Hold'em.* He's played seven-card stud and both limit and no-limit hold'em everywhere from the underground clubs of New York City to the casino poker rooms on the Vegas strip. He lives in Hastings-on-Hudson, New York.